6(

000(

Brief Therapy and Eating Disorders

A Practical Guide to Solution-Focused Work with Clients

Jossey-Bass Publishers • San Francisco

Substantial discounts on bulk quantities of Jossey-Bass books are
available to corporations, professional associations, and other
organizations. For details and discount information, contact the
special sales department at Jossey-Bass Inc., Publishers.
(415) 433–1740; Fax (800) 605–2665.

For sales outside the United States, please contact your local
Paramount Publishing International Office.

 Manufactured in the United States of America on Lyons Falls
Pathfinder Tradebook. This paper is acid-free and 100 percent
totally chlorine-free.

Library of Congress Cataloging-in-Publication Data

McFarland, Barbara.
    Brief therapy and eating disorders : a practical guide to
solution-focused work with clients / [Barbara McFarland].—1st ed.
       p.   cm.—(Joint publication in the Jossey-Bass social and
behavioral sciences series and the Jossey-Bass health series)
    Includes bibliographical references and index.
    ISBN 0-7879-0053-2
    1. Eating disorders—treatment. 2. Solution-focused
therapy. 3. Brief psychotherapy. I. Title. II. Series: Jossey-Bass
social and behavioral sciences series. III. Series: Jossey-Bass
health series
    RC552.E18M388   1995
    616.85'260651—dc20
                                    94-38947
                                        CIP

FIRST EDITION
HB Printing   10 9 8 7 6 5 4 3 2 1   *Code 9510*

A joint publication in

The Jossey-Bass Social and Behavioral

Science Series

and

The Jossey-Bass Health Series

To "ever the best of friends,"
my spouse, Harold,
and my son, Casey

Contents

Resources: Self-Reporting Forms

Preface

As third-party payers demand economy and quality in mental health services, clinicians are faced with ever-increasing pressures to treat clients as cost effectively as possible. Due to the clinical complexity of the eating disorder syndromes, this demand is a particular challenge to clinicians who treat anorexia nervosa and bulimia nervosa. In order to be effective practitioners in this era of health care reform and increasingly stringent managed care guidelines, clinicians need to be open to brief therapy models and the skills that accompany these models. One particular model that is highly effective with eating disorder clients is the solution-focused brief therapy model as developed by Steve deShazer and his colleagues at the Brief Family Therapy Center in Milwaukee, Wisconsin.

Audience

This book will be of interest to psychologists, psychiatrists, EAP counselors, chemical dependency counselors, mental health and substance abuse agency clinicians, academics who teach clinicians, and those with eating disorders who want to know more about how they might be helped.

Overview of the Contents

Brief Therapy and Eating Disorders: A Practical Guide to Solution Focused Work with Clients was written to help clinicians who treat eating disorder clients develop the skills and techniques needed to face the challenges posed by health care reform. A practical hands-on tool, this book is intended to increase the reader's skill as an effective brief therapist. In it, I present an overview of the current clinical trends in the field and an in-depth exploration of the basic tenets of the solution-focused model as it applies to eating disorders. Then I discuss specific solution-focused interviewing techniques and strategies, illustrating them with numerous case studies and transcriptions of therapeutic interviews with eating disorder clients.

In addition to exploring specific solution-focused techniques used in treating clients individually, I also discuss the solution-focused, structured outpatient group treatment program currently practiced at my clinic, Eating Disorders Recovery Center in Cincinnati, Ohio.

In Chapter One, I describe how I came to specialize in treating eating disorder clients and how I began learning about brief therapy out of necessity and then discovered its many virtues. The conceptual shift it requires clinicians to make, from focusing on the causes of symptoms to uncovering solutions in the patient's own experience has turned out to be a successful and productive change of direction. I also discuss self-efficacy theory (Bandura, 1977) in relation to the solution-focused model, emphasizing that increasing the client's perceptions of self-efficacy is a major goal in therapy. Chapter Two summarizes current treatment approaches from a historical perspective, outlining four waves of influence in the field, the fourth wave being solution-focused brief therapy.

Chapter Three addresses the basic principles and assumptions that underlie the solution-focused brief therapy model and that will guide the clinician in implementing it. These assumptions are discussed in relation to eating disorders treatment. Chapter Four explores the key qualities of the therapeutic relationship within the solution-focused model. From this theoretical foundation,

I integrate deShazer's (1988) solution-focused types of the therapeutic relationship with the clients' stages of change as developed by Prochaska and DiClemente (1982). Because eating disorder clients have a high drop-out rate, I also apply the solution-focused framework to this population, and in so doing, I assist the therapist in significantly increasing levels of client cooperation.

Those who have written about solution-oriented therapy tend to conceive of the therapeutic interviewing process as a *therapeutic conversation* during which the therapist actively assists the client in accurately defining the problem and searching for solutions salient to that client (Anderson & Goolishian, 1988; Weakland, 1993). The types of questions asked by the therapist are critical not only to the accomplishment of treatment goals but also to the communication of the therapist's beliefs about the therapeutic process. Therefore, in Chapter Five I present the solution-focused methods of interviewing developed to shape the client's perception of the problem in a way that leads to solutions (Berg & Miller, 1992). I also present a structure for the solution-focused first session interview.

Chapter Six presents specific strategies and solution-focused techniques that have been particularly useful with eating disorder clients, especially the more challenging cases. The chapter describes interventions, interviewing questions, and homework assignments that are employed to help the client expand upon the problem behavior exceptions that she or he has identified.

Chapter Seven describes the solution-focused, structured group treatment program at the Eating Disorders Recovery Center, including the center's solution-focused body image groups and psychoeducational groups. Each component of the program is presented in detail. Chapter Eight is a brief epilogue.

The core documents used at the Eating Disorders Recovery Center for patient self-reporting, self-assessment, and goal setting appear in Resources A, B, C, D, E, and F.

Acknowledgments

This book is a composite of the influence of a great many people. I have been fortunate enough to work directly with many skilled therapists, such as Scott Miller, Lynn Johnson, and Steven Friedman, as well as Yvonne Dolan, Insoo Kim Berg, Carina Schlanger, and Paul Watzlawick, in whose workshops I have participated. All these individuals have been extremely instrumental in my development as a solution-focused brief therapist. Others I have come to know through their books. The most influential of these authors have been Bill O'Hanlon and Steve deShazer.

Through many discussions, the staff of the Eating Disorders Recovery Center and the Brief Therapy Center have helped me to crystallize my thinking regarding brief therapy and to implement the solution-focused model in my clinical work with eating disorder clients. The clients at the Eating Disorders Recovery Center and the Brief Therapy Center have graciously allowed center therapists to videotape sessions so we could continue refining our skills.

I extend a special note of appreciation to Lynn Johnson, who not only provided invaluable feedback on parts of the manuscript but also was extremely supportive of the project; to Tyeis Baker Baumann, my colleague of ten years, who provided assistance and feedback on Chapter Seven; to Peggy Sheets, my clinical assistant, who amidst a variety of other tasks diligently transcribed videotapes; to Colleen Byrne, my research assistant, who cheerfully trudged to the library; to Jim Heisel, my colleague and training partner, for his timely words of encouragement and feedback; to Adrienne Dressel Graff, my dear friend and cousin, for believing in me; and last but not least, to my spouse, Harold, for his feedback on technical aspects of the manuscript as well as for his unending support and patience during its development.

January 1995

Barbara McFarland
Cincinnati, Ohio

The Author

Barbara McFarland is founder of the Eating Disorders Recovery Center and the Brief Therapy Center of Cincinnati. She has fourteen year's clinical experience working primarily with women suffering from eating disorders. In addition to her private practice, she conducts national training workshops on solution-based brief therapy and works extensively toward sensitizing and educating managed care and health care administrators on the necessity of re-training clinicians in brief therapy in order to maximize quality of care within health care reform guidelines. McFarland has written numerous articles and several books on eating disorders, including *Shame and Body Image*, *Feeding the Empty Heart*, and *Abstinence in Action*.

She lives with her spouse, Harold, on their farm in Burlington, Kentucky.

Brief Therapy and Eating Disorders

One

Introduction: Using Solution-Focused Brief Therapy with Eating Disorder Clients

The two most significant events that have altered the course of my professional career have been serendipitous rather than planned. These two milestones in my life exposed me first to eating disorders and then to solution-focused brief therapy.

My initial clinical experience with a bulimic occurred in 1978, when I was a clinical consulting psychologist for CareUnit Hospital in Cincinnati, Ohio. Given the unique recovery issues that alcoholic women (the term *chemically dependent* was not in vogue at that time) must contend with—sexual abuse, physical abuse, economic dependence, and so forth—I had decided to form both a psychotherapy group and an aftercare group for alcoholic female patients on the unit. Something quite unheard of back then.

At one group session, a woman whom I will call "Kate" approached me somewhat reluctantly and very sheepishly asked if I had time to see her individually. As it happened, another woman I was scheduled to see had taken ill, so I was available right at that hour. With eyes downcast and in what was barely a whisper, Kate then revealed, with a great many pregnant pauses, that she frequently would eat huge quantities of food in secret and then make herself throw up. As she uttered these last words, she looked at me intently, scrutinizing my reaction to her well-kept secret. Since I had no prior experience with such symptomatology, I was somewhat nonplussed by her disclosure, but I must have communicated a level of acceptance because she launched into the story of her painful relationship with food and her dieting and vomiting. (As we spoke,

1

I recalled that at our last staff meeting, the evening nurses had been baffled by the mysterious disappearance of food!) Kate graduated from the CareUnit program the next day and religiously attended my aftercare group, but she never mentioned another word about her "secret." Nevertheless, I was so intrigued by her eating and purging behaviors that I marched over to the hospital library where I discovered some articles on anorexia but nothing much that described Kate's binging and purging behavior.

A year later, I was asked to join the staff of Eden Treatment Center for Women as a clinical consulting psychologist. Eden House, as it was locally referred to, was a residential treatment center for indigent alcoholic women. My main responsibilities were to revise the entire treatment program and to conduct therapy groups with the residents. Once again, at a staff meeting the night manager complained that a considerable amount of food was mysteriously missing. As the staff made wild speculations about its disappearance, I shared with them my experience at the CareUnit. They looked at me with incredulity; however, after further discussion, I suggested that I be allowed to present a didactic to the residents on addiction and food and to tell Kate's story. I came up with this idea as a result of something Kate had repeated over and over again: "This thing I have with food is much worse than my alcoholism. I am hooked. You can live without alcohol, but how the hell do you live without food?"

On the day I delivered the lecture, two women approached me separately in therapy sessions and reticently revealed that they frequently binged and purged. Those sessions initiated my clinical work in eating disorders. A few years later, I opened the Eating Disorders Recovery Center which provided structured group and individual treatment specifically for anorexia, bulimia, and compulsive eating. The disease model of addiction was the philosophical base of the program.

At the time it occurred, my second career-altering event seemed more foreboding than serendipitous. In 1991, I was fast becoming irritated by the demands insurance companies were making regarding treatment plans, treatment plan reviews, and telephone authorizations. I considered these demands something I had to endure and viewed them simply as more bureaucracy. One day, however, a colleague who managed a behavioral health care group that referred clients extensively to my center informed me, in confidence, that I had been identified as an outlier. Consequently, his group would no longer be able to refer clients to me. He said the next step would be my actual termination from one of the largest managed care networks in town unless I decreased my utilization numbers. He advised me to start being more cost effective in the delivery of my services.

My general malaise in relation to managed care was now supplanted by a sense of extreme urgency. I began to educate myself about the realities of managed care and its impact on delivery of services. As I increased my understanding of clinical trends, I realized I did have to learn how to be a more efficient therapist. Where once I could treat patients as long as the patient and I both felt it was necessary, I now understood that ten treatment sessions was considered lengthy. This treatment restriction was particularly disturbing to me because eating disorder clients are frequently at greater medical risk than most other mental health clients and are often members of highly dysfunctional family systems. I was in a quandary as to how this clinical population could be treated briefly!

The Case for Brief Therapy

To me *brief therapy* was an oxymoron. Turning once again to the library stacks, I discovered that there are various models of brief therapy and that it may be psychodynamically, behaviorally, or cognitively based. Also, no one seemed to agree on the length of brief treatment, and the literature indicated ranges from one to twenty-five sessions. After much study and countless discussions with brief therapists, I learned that *brief* is a misnomer, since the number of sessions is irrelevant to the actual practice of brief therapy. Basically, brief therapy can be defined as *no more therapy than necessary*.

In addition, the goals of brief therapy tend to be more limited than traditional therapy. According to Koss & Butcher (1986), "most brief therapists strive to accomplish one or more of the following goals: removal or amelioration of the patient's most disabling symptoms as rapidly as possible; prompt reestablishment of the patient's previous emotional equilibrium; and development of the patient's understanding of the current disturbance and increased coping ability in the future" (p. 642).

In brief therapy, the role of the therapist is more directive and active than in traditional therapy, and the therapist and the patient specifically negotiate what the focus of treatment will be. Thus, in contrast to traditional therapy, which focuses on interpretation and seeks to help the client gain understanding, brief therapy is highly goal driven, focuses on directives, and seeks to produce change.

During the course of my research into brief therapy, one approach in particular challenged the clinical paradigm I had been trained in. This approach was *solution-focused brief therapy*, and it seemed especially stimulating. Developed by Steve deShazer and his colleagues at the Brief Family Therapy Center in Milwaukee, the solution-focused model is nonpathological, focusing instead on client strengths, resources, and competencies.

The more I learned about this model, the more it seemed analogous to alternative healing in medicine. Much like homeopathic medicine, which respects the natural healing powers of the body, solution-focused brief therapy respects the natural problem-solving abilities or solution patterns of the client. The therapist does no more than facilitate the process. The idea of applying this model to eating disorders intrigued me. After that, not only did my staff and I attend every solution-focused workshop we could find but we also had Scott Miller, a staff member at the Brief Family Therapy Center, train and supervise us frequently. Also, I was fortunate enough to receive supervision from solution-oriented brief therapists Steven

Friedman and Lynn Johnson. My initial doubts about brief therapy were soon supplanted by a respectful admiration for its effectiveness. Over the past two years, my staff and I have applied the model to our eating disorder clients both in individual treatment and in our structured group treatment program. To refine our work, we have studied hundreds of videotapes of our individual sessions with clients, and we continue to do so.

This book outlines the results of my clinical experiences and observations with eating disorder clients using the solution-focused brief therapy model. My staff and I have made many discoveries about the resiliency of clients whom we once saw as broken. Where we once held the belief espoused in much of the clinical literature that this population is difficult to treat, we now feel hopeful. In the past two years, we have gradually but dramatically altered the principles and philosophy of our entire treatment program and treatment approach. Although our treatment is not "pure" solution-focused brief therapy, it is strongly influenced by that model. Our length-of-stay statistics have decreased dramatically, and follow-up study results are similar to results for both the Mental Research Institute in Palo Alto, California, and the Brief Family Therapy Center.

For example, in June of 1993, the Eating Disorders Recovery Center (EDRC) telephoned twenty-four patients who had participated in individual therapy to ask them about their results. These patients had terminated treatment from six months to one year before this survey; their average number of sessions during treatment was 7.1. Eighty-four percent of the respondents said their counseling goals had been met; 66 percent said that their situation had gotten "better," and 71 percent said other areas of their lives had improved. Seventy-nine percent had not sought other counseling since the brief therapy counseling. Thirty-three percent indicated that their work had improved (62 percent indicated improved attitude; 37 percent, improved attendance; and 62 percent, improved performance), while 20 percent thought their work had not improved (47 percent said the question was not applicable). Asked whether their health was "any better," 54 percent responded affirmatively and 21 percent negatively (25 percent said the question was not applicable). Seventy-seven percent reported not having to see a physician for other than routine medical examinations.

Given the current stringent reimbursement environment in which health care providers must function, clinicians face great challenges in treating eating disorder clients within a limited time frame. In mental health and substance abuse treatment today, there are many diverse gatekeepers, such as employee assistance counselors, managed care case managers, and all the others who serve as conduits between those seeking clinical services and those who provide them. In the past, clinicians have had only one customer to satisfy—the client. Now, we have to contend with a diverse array of customers including managed care companies, employee assistance programs, and primary care physicians, to mention a few. Those of us who provide clinical services need to aggressively market and promote ourselves to these various gatekeepers. However, clinicians who want a competitive advantage in the marketplace must also be able to meet the following criteria:

- Demonstrated competency in brief therapy, as reflected in length-of-stay statistics
- Published measures of outcomes that include both client satisfaction surveys and clinical outcomes
- Heightened sensitivity to the ongoing issues in health care reform
- Demonstrated shared commitment to cost containment and total quality, exhibited through effective written and oral communication

Since eating disorders are considered a specialized field in mental health, those clinicians or institutions who have established structured outpatient eating disorder programs in their communities will have a greater chance of surviving health care reforms. However, their survival will also be highly contingent upon their ability to meet the above criteria.

The major objective of managed care companies is to provide the least intrusive, most cost-effective treatment first. Inpatient programs for eating disorder patients will be unable to survive in this environment and many are already closing their doors or evolving into partial hospitalization programs. However, managed care companies view even the latter programs as expensive and secondary to intensive outpatient therapy. Because stabilization followed by outpatient therapy is rapidly becoming the standard reimbursable treatment protocol for eating disorder patients, clinicians must be prepared to effectively treat these clients within the stringent managed care guidelines.

For clinicians to become efficient, each one must reexamine the longstanding assumption of the mental health field that says treatment gains are contingent upon the length of psychotherapy. We have long held to this notion that the more psychotherapy the better off the patient will be. The research, however, does not support our premise. One outcome research study (Smith, Glass, & Miller, 1980), for example, found that the greatest gains in psychotherapy occurred within the first six to eight sessions, followed by continuing but diminishing gains for roughly the next ten sessions. Similar findings by Orlinsky and Howard (1986) also suggested "diminishing returns" after six to eight sessions, "with more and more effort required to achieve just noticeable difference in patient improvement" (p. 361). Other research generally supports this finding. In addition, this time frame matches the amount of time for which most patients expect to receive treatment services (Garfield, 1971, 1978).

According to Budman and Gurman (1988), who review the literature on time-limited therapy, the research shows there are no reliable differences in clinical effectiveness between time-limited and time-unlimited therapy. In fact, Budman and Gurman believe that, at times, clients who receive time-limited therapy actually obtain more treatment than clients in time-unlimited therapy, because "the essence of brief psychotherapy lies not in its numerical time characteristics, but in the therapeutic values, attitudes and aims of the therapist" (p. 9).

Traditional Versus Solution-Focused Treatment

There are three camps in the treatment of eating disorders: one espouses the necessity of reaching a psychodynamic understanding of symptoms, another concentrates on direct symptom management, and yet another deals with altering family interactional patterns. These divergent clinical perspectives have resulted in conflicting points of view on fundamental issues.

Historically viewed, the eating disorders field has experienced three waves of clinical influence, each wave representing one of the major camps of treatment. Solution-oriented models signal the emergence of a fourth wave characterized by a dramatic clinical shift that requires both client and therapist to go beyond seeking to understand the problem. That is, rather than continuing to look for causes, the fourth wave of treatment presses for the development of solutions that take advantage of competencies and resiliencies inherent in the client. It offers a unique perspective of identifying exceptions to the problem behavior and using those exceptions as patterns for a solution, a solution that has already been working for the client even though in a limited fashion. To apply this unique perspective, clinicians must be willing to accept and paradigm shift. Making the shift in paradigms compelled me to stop asking the questions, What's wrong with this client? and, Why is the client doing this? and to start asking, What does this client want? and, How can things be better in the future? Exploring the whys of the behaviors and taking deep excursions into the past were no longer helpful in creating rapid change and, more importantly, in empowering clients to recognize and appreciate their own personal efficacy and resourcefulness.

Even though many of the sequelae of eating disorders are alleviated by eating, weight, and diet normalization, the long-term consequences of eating disorders remain obscure. For those individuals who seek therapeutic intervention, it can only be assumed that their experience leaves them not only with heightened awarenesses and skills for living but also with a sense of their own capabilities and future possibilities. I believe wholeheartedly that this positive result is only feasible through a solution-focused model. By focusing on clients' deficits and limitations with the aim of "fixing" the clients or making them "whole" again, the pathology-based paradigm of traditional mental health treatment promotes a sense of personal inadequacy. Eating disorder clients are particularly vulnerable to this viewpoint, since they generally see themselves as innately defective and often report feeling a deep sense of personal shame.

Eating disorder clients are also generally known to be "experts" in nutrition as a result of their anorexia or bulimia; equally, they are experts in trying to determine the reason why they have their enigmatic behaviors, and they spend considerable amounts of cognitive energy looking for the one answer that will rid them of their malediction. Therapy should not keep them entangled in the web of their own plight but rather should facilitate a reawakening of their inner resourcefulness to help them search for realistic and achievable solutions. Physician Andrew Weil (1988) says that it is a misnomer to call medicine "the healing art," because "the healing art is the secret wisdom of the body. Medicine can do no more than facilitate it" (p. 76). So too, the client has a secret wisdom that psychotherapy can only hope to uncover.

Bill O'Hanlon (1993) discusses a similar sort of facilitation as he looks at iatrogenic injury and iatrogenic healing in the mental health field in relation to what he calls *possibility therapy*. *Iatrogenic*, which comes from Greek *iatros* ("physician") and *genic* ("caused by"), refers to the results caused by the practice of medicine. It is often used about negative results and was initially applied only to the medical healing arts. Applying the concept to the mental health field, O'Hanlon defines iatrogenic injury as *those methods, techniques, assessment procedures, explanations, or interventions that harm, discourage, invalidate, show disrespect or close down the possibilities for change*" [italics mine]. Iatrogenic healing consists of "those methods, techniques, assessment procedures, explanations or interventions that encourage, are respectful and open up the possibilities for change" (p. 4).

I believe that clinicians who treat eating disorder clients need to be especially skilled at promoting iatrogenic healing. Too often in our attempts to be helpful with this very challenging and heterogenous population, we over-assess, overdiagnose, and overtreat our clients. Even though managed care has been somewhat of a burden, I believe it has forced clinicians to supplant their disease-based paradigm with a model that focuses on health, resourcefulness, and wellness.

What participants in my workshops deem most noteworthy is that the solution-focused approach is very positive. However, it is important, as O'Hanlon cautions, not to be too simplistic about this positive aspect. Solution-oriented brief therapy approaches are not to be confused with the motivational "positive thinking" ideology so prevalent in our culture. O'Hanlon's possibility therapy, or possibility thinking, "does not claim that everything is (or will be) wonderful and successful or that it is (or will be) awful and futile. . . . The possibility therapist recognizes the seriousness of clients' situations without taking a minimizing or Pollyanna view" (p. 5). That *non*simplistic approach is essentially the view I have taken in this book.

At the same time, *Brief Therapy and Eating Disorders* is intended to be a very practical hands-on guide for "doing" solution-focused brief therapy with eating disorder clients. As I reviewed and read the literature on eating disorders, I was overwhelmed by the sheer amount of information and the vast numbers of investigations on etiology, epidemiology, and pathogenesis, matched by an equally vast number of writings addressing the various psychotherapeutic modalities employed in the treatment of anorexia and bulimia. Given this variety of theory as well as the realities of actual practice, it is not surprising that clinicians often feel an overwhelming sense of despair or frustration when treating eating disorder clients.

Since clinicians are now also dealing with the pressures and frustrations related to health care reforms, it seems logical to look to simplify the clinical approach in two ways: first, by allowing the client to determine treatment goals, and second, by initially using the least intrusive therapeutic interventions and only increasing their complexity gradually and as needed. Treating clients in this parsimonious manner has a twofold benefit: it is efficient, but what is even more important, it validates the client as a capable and worthwhile human being.

The literature consistently emphasizes that eating disorder clients suffer from low self-esteem (Boskind-Lodahl, 1976; Johnson & Maddi, 1986; Love, Ollendick, Johnson, & Schlesinger, 1985; Root, Fallon, & Friedrich, 1986; Slade, 1982; Striegel-Moore, Silberstein, & Rodin, 1986; Swift, Bushnell, Hanson, & Logemann, 1986); low self-esteem related to body image and dieting (Cash, Winstead, & Janda, 1986; Heatherton & Polivy, 1992; Rosen, Gross, & Vara, 1987); intense feelings of shame related to self and body (McFarland & Baker-Baumann, 1990); and "a paralyzing sense of ineffectiveness" (Bruch, 1973, p.13). The solution-focused model provides a specific path for the therapist to help the client increase perceptions of self-efficacy and self-esteem. I believe this focus on self-efficacy is the pivotal treatment issue for clients who suffer from an eating disorder. It is the view that fosters efficiency and is the least intrusive treatment, since the determinants of self-efficacy are identified by the client rather than the therapist (looking through his or her particular philosophical orientation).

✓ *Self-efficacy*, defined as "how well one can execute courses of action required to deal with prospective situations" (Bandura, 1982b, p. 122), is related to feelings of competence and power or control. A person who perceives herself as efficacious in tasks that are highly valued by her generally feels competent and in control, and thus experiences a more positive level of self-esteem. Conversely, the inability to feel a sense of personal agency or control in one's life often generates strong feelings of futility and despondency.

Self-efficacy theory distinguishes between two types of judgments regarding futility (Bandura, 1982b): people give up trying because they are beleaguered by self-doubt over their capabilities or, even though they are assured of their capabilities, they give up because they expect their efforts will produce no results (Bandura, 1982b). Those individuals who have a low sense of self-efficacy and experience no rewards as a result of their efforts become depressed and despondent (Bandura, 1982b), and thus are more prone to experience low self-esteem. This judgment of failure is particularly debilitating when the individual attributes it to personal deficiencies and has stringent standards of self-evaluation—two key factors that characterize the eating disorder client.

Repeatedly failing and feeling out of control, powerless, and incompetent in relation to a task that the individual values highly can only serve to weaken an already fragile sense of self-worth and promote a disparaging self-view. On the other hand, succeeding in mastering a task that is valued highly promotes feelings of control, competency, and empowerment and thus positively affects one's self-view.

✓ Because of their dietary failures, eating disorder clients perceive their self-efficacy to be greatly weakened or shaken. Research suggests that people's levels of self-esteem have an impact on their eating behaviors (Polivy, Heatherton, & Herman, 1988). These investigators demonstrated that high self-esteem is associated with less disinhibited eating, and that repeated dietary failures take their toll on the self-esteem of some dieters. They speculate that disinhibited eating lowers the dieter's self-esteem making the dieter more vulnerable to disinhibited eating in the future. This can result in what the investigators refer to as a *self-perpetuating spiral,* in which the individual is psychologically and biologically locked in a self-perpetuating negative pattern.

Repeated dieting serves to perpetuate this pervasive sense of inefficacy because an increased efficiency in metabolic response makes weight loss a more difficult task not only to achieve but to maintain. Thus, the individual becomes more desperate in her attempts to increase her sense of personal competency and sense of control through her weight loss efforts.

The issue of self-esteem and the role it plays in eating disorders are pivotal factors in the treatment process. For many bulimics, self-efficacy is deeply impaired over the course of many attempts to control behavior, which only serves to reinforce the bulimics' perceived inadequacies. This negative feedback loop, in conjunction with the physiological ramifications of dieting, perpetuates an abysmal sense of helplessness and despair. This pervasive sense of ineffectiveness keeps the individual trapped in the binge/purge cycle.

An individual's percepts of self-efficacy are steppingstones in determining the quality of her self-esteem and serve to mediate behavior (DiClemente, Prochaska, & Gibertini, 1985). When an individual perceives herself as efficacious in tasks or situations that she values highly, she generally feels a sense of competence and thus experiences a more positive level of self-esteem. Because the eating disorder client's perception of self-efficacy is greatly diminished, a major goal of treatment should be to increase the client's percepts related to her level of self-efficacy, particularly in the areas of her dietary practices and purging activities. By focusing on the client's own mastery experiences related to the eating/restricting/purging behaviors, further entrenchment in the maladaptive behaviors is thwarted or reduced, and the individual is likely to experience a positive ripple effect that will influence other aspects of her life. This is accomplished primarily by amplifying, reinforcing, and highlighting exceptions and solution patterns and by establishing proximal goals that are salient to the client. Specific techniques of exploring exceptions and solution patterns and developing salient goals for the client will be explored in great detail in Chapters Five and Six.

Maslow (1966) warns against operating from a single orientation or perspective, stating, "If the only tool you have is a hammer . . . [you tend] to treat everything as if it were a nail" (pp. 15–16). Although the solution-focused approach is only one tool, it initiates a new clinical trend in the eating disorders field by emphasizing the significance of highlighting and reenforcing client competencies. The remainder of this book will explore this issue.

A Note on Terminology

I now find diagnostic labels detrimental to the therapeutic process, and I no longer label clients as anorexics or bulimics in my practice (although I do have my lapses). Instead, I have clients who seek treatment for complaints related to binging behaviors, erratic dietary patterns, restricting behaviors, purging behaviors, or activities such as laxative abuse, excessive exercise behaviors, vomiting, and so on. However, I have used the labels *anorexic* and *bulimic*, as well as *eating disorder client*, in this book, since that is still the common terminology in most practices and the literature.

Also, because a large majority of eating disorder clients are female, I use "she" when referring to individual clients throughout this book, although the techniques I describe will work with male clients, too.

Two

Shifting Paradigms: Beyond Sickness

"We're all mad here. I'm mad. You're mad."

"How do you know I'm mad?" said Alice.

"You must be," said the Cat, "or you wouldn't have come here."

Alice didn't think that proved it at all.

—*Lewis Carroll*
Alice's Adventures in Wonderland

Trying to fully understand the eating disorders is like trying to untie the Gordian knot. Clinical writings reveal that, given the diversity and complexity of the behaviors and the heterogeneity of the population, there is no single, specific etiology for the eating disorders. Instead, researchers postulate multiple variables that interactively serve as potential pathogenic routes and increase the risk of an individual's developing an eating disorder. The more commonly accepted risk factors can be summed up under four kinds of variables.

Sociocultural Variables

- The thin body ideal is valued and the thin body is seen as symbolizing self-discipline, control, independence, and attractiveness.
- Physical appearance of the body is a measure of female attractiveness and social success.
- Women's role expectations are in conflict: the Superwoman complex.

Familial Variables

- Family is highly achievement oriented and perfectionist.
- Family places great emphasis on appearance and is preoccupied with food, dieting, and bodily functions.
- Family tends to exhibit rigidity, enmeshment, inability to resolve conflicts, and overprotectiveness.
- First- and second-degree relatives have above average incidence of depression and bipolar illnesses, chemical dependency problems, and eating disorders.
- Dysfunctional family communication patterns often result in coalitions among members.

Individual Variables

- The person is an adolescent female who is slightly overweight.
- The person has impaired self-concept and general feelings of ineffectiveness.
- The person has difficulty adapting to the maturational tasks of adolescence.
- The person has marked cognitive distortions related to shape and weight.
- The person has an impaired body image and distorted internal cues related to hunger.
- The person has dysphoria, affective instability, or impulsivity.
- The person tends toward an obsessional style.
- The person engages in repeated attempts at dieting.

Biological Variables

- The person has menstrual irregularity.
- The person is female (gender).
- The dysregulation of serotonin results in binge eating of high carbohydrate foods.

- The mechanism of satiety (cholecystokinin) is impaired.
- The person has other chemical imbalances in the brain.
- The effects of starvation alter mood, cognitive ability, and character traits, causing the eating disorder to become more entrenched and resistant to treatment.
- Restrictive dieting adversely affects satiety cues, which are correlating with binge behaviors, and metabolic rate, which can promote weight gain.
- Strict dieting and exercise can trigger the biobehavioral processes which result in anorexia.

The eating disorder field is replete with speculations regarding the etiology and pathogenesis of the syndromes. The enigma surrounding the eating disorders has only fueled the fascination of researchers and clinicians alike. What seems even more seductive is that there are opportunities for everyone, from anthropologists to physiologists to pharmacologists to philosophers. Sometimes, the quest to understand these disorders has seemed to be at a point where it is only creating more uncertainty and doubt about the "real" nature of the syndromes.

Although the field is still in its infancy, its clinical development reaching back only sixty years, there have already been significant theoretical shifts and clinical transformations that are continuing to unfold today; the most significant of these transformations is the subject of this book.

Four Waves of Clinical Influence

Since the 1930s, each of four waves of clinical influence has contributed significantly toward refining clinical practice in treating anorexia nervosa and bulimia nervosa. The first wave of influence identified anorexia as a psychological condition requiring psychiatric intervention. This wave was heavily dominated by psychoanalytic thinking, and treatment centered on the disturbed eating function, or the oral component, of the disorder. Thus, clinicians were of the opinion that anorexia nervosa was symbolic of fixated unconscious conflicts relating to oral-sadistic fears, oral impregnation, and other regressive wishes and primitive fantasies (Waller, Kaufman, & Deutsch, 1940.)

Hilde Bruch (1970, 1973, 1977, 1978, 1985) was the seminal contributor to the psychoanalytical conceptualization of eating disorders in the last three decades. As a result of her extensive clinical experience in the treatment of long-term anorexic patients, Bruch came to question whether drive dynamics and intrapsychic conflicts were as specific to the disorder as postulated. She emphasized pre-Oedipal development, observing that anorexic patients demonstrated significant deficiencies in their self-identity and autonomy. The first wave, then, is punctuated by Hilde Bruch's contributions, which extrapolated from "pure" psychoanalytic theory an emphasis on the functional and adaptational effects of starvation in response to pervasive feelings of ineffectiveness, passivity, and control by external forces.

Feminist psychoanalytic and self-psychology approaches also emerged as extrapolations of the psychoanalytic approach and contributed to the thinking of the first wave. The major treatment objective was to correct the characterological deficits of the client as they related to the development of the "self."

The main characteristics of the first wave are listed in the following summary.

First Wave: Psychodynamic Approach
(Seeks to answer the question, Why is this a problem?
Focuses on distal influences)

Identified problem: Separation/individuation from pre-Oedipal
                        mother.
Goal of therapy: Repair characterological deficits in order to
                        assist client to develop a separate sense of self.

Catalyst for change: Therapeutic relationship.

Place of change: Therapy session/therapist's office.

Task of therapist: Provide and teach tension regulation and integration by using the leverage of idealization.

Role of therapist: Teacher, mirror, guide, parent, advisor.

Role of client: Passive recipient of care.

The second wave of treatment introduced cognitive and cognitive/behavioral approaches intended to alter the client's distorted or faulty cognitive sets related to maladaptive eating/purging patterns. These orientations actually introduced the practice of brief, focused therapy into the eating disorders field. The clinical efficacy of such group treatment approaches and the nature of the disorders themselves have done more to shape the treatment protocol to be focused, specific, and time limited.

This particular wave greatly contributed to techniques of altering starvation-binge-purge cycles in systematic ways that were used extensively in both inpatient and outpatient programs The second wave also had two subphases: multimodal treatment programs and pharmacological approaches. During the 1970s, myriad inpatient and outpatient programs emerged to meet the growing numbers of clients and significant others seeking treatment for the eating disorders. The clinical contributions of these programs over the last twenty years have served to emphasize the benefits of a multidimensional therapeutic approach that integrates divergent theoretical and management tenets. However, although eclectic in format, each multimodal program is usually driven by a particular theoretical orientation, which serves as the core of the treatment services. Typically, psychodynamic approaches serve as this therapeutic core.

Pharmacological approaches, the other subphase of the second wave, emerged to address the chemical imbalances that have been hypothesized to cause disturbed eating and binging patterns.

Medications in eating disorders, as in other psychiatric conditions, are considered most effective when used in conjunction with some type of therapy.

Second Wave: Cognitive/Behavioral Approach
(Seeks to answer the question, How can symptomatic behaviors be altered? Focuses on proximal influences)

Identified problem: Faulty cognitions related to eating, weight, and body shape.

Goal of therapy: Explore and identify immediate precipitating or consequent influences on the restricting, binging, and purging behaviors; focus on symptoms.

Catalyst for change: Techniques or procedures that promote the modification of cognitive structures.

Place of change: Inside therapy; outside therapy—as a result of homework assignments.

Task of therapist: Examine distortions and misperceptions related to food, weight, body shape, and interpersonal world.

Role of therapist: Teacher, guide, advisor.

Role of client: Participant in process.

The third wave stirred family systems into the potpourri of clinical approaches. Family systems therapists seek to change the interactional patterns within the client system and, thus, focus on the individual within the context of her family relationships. This approach has been influential in shifting the focus of treatment from the individual client to include her family system. For a time, any treatment program that did not include intensive family therapy as a central part of its therapeutic regimen was viewed dubiously, although solution-focused therapy is less rigorous on this topic.

Traditional psychology and psychiatry were based on analyzing past events in order to understand the client's present problems and produce the changes necessary to reach a solution. In the 1950s, however, a different epistemology emerged, based on the concept of information. This epistemology is the bedrock of the third wave of influence in the field, and it views causality as circular and centers on the communication patterns of systems, or global patterns. It was Gregory Bateson and Don Jackson who helped develop this epistemology by shifting principles of cybernetics and anthropology to the study of families with a dysfunctional family member. Consequently, some if not all psychotherapeutic approaches moved from an intrapsychic to a relational, or contextual, approach. New questions were asked as the focus shifted from, Why is this a problem within this individual? to, How is this problem being maintained within this individual's family system?

There are two basic models for the systems approach: the structural, systemic view (Haley, 1967, 1973; Madanes, 1981; Minuchin, Rosman, & Baker, 1978) and the focused problem-solving view, or interactional view, which was the model used by the Mental Research Institute (MRI) founded by Don Jackson in 1959. Both basic models were significantly influenced by the work of Bateson and Erickson. The further development of the MRI model has been largely carried out by John Weakland, Richard Fisch, and Paul Watzlawick, and their colleagues (Weakland, Fisch, Watzlawick, & Bodin, 1974).

Systemic therapists (Haley and his colleagues) view the main issue for the client as the hierarchical incongruities within the family system, incongruities that result in power plays and coalitions. For Haley, symptoms are the metaphor for the problem, while the client sees the symptoms as a pseudosolution. Treatment focuses on the management of power within the family and on a reconfiguration of the family hierarchy. The role of the therapist is to restructure the family's power game in order to restore the family to a more functional mode of operation (Haley, 1976a). Selvini-Palazzoli (1978) is a proponent of a more classical systemic approach and has applied that model to the treatment of eating disorders. Minuchin (Minuchin, Rosman, & Baker, 1978) addresses problem maintenance as a result of various family organizational patterns and coalitions. This model is not interested in treating the individual alone but as she exists in her significant social contexts, so that when important family interactional patterns are altered, meaningful changes take place in the symptomatology. Selvini-Palazzoli focuses on the communication patterns within the system as the focus of treatment. Both systemic approaches energized the eating disorders field and served as a catalyst for the development of other systemically based family models.

The interactive MRI model attempts to understand what specific changes the client desires in solving the complaint and what specific methods she is using to solve the problem, and then attempts to alter the problem-solving process by suggesting the client do the opposite of what she has been doing. In other words, the client's attempted solutions are viewed as the problem, and thus, the focus of treatment is not the complaint but these solutions.

According to deShazer (1991, p. 55), where the structural view assumes that clients' problems are a reflection of a wrong or dysfunctional social organization and intervention is based on a map of what is supposedly a correct family hierarchy, the focused problem-solving model (MRI model) assumes that clients are doing the best they can and further assumes that family hierarchy or structure is not important in doing therapy. They do not assume a pathological, illness, or disease-oriented view of the family or family structure, rather they focus on sequences of interaction and problem-solving behavior.

Third Wave: Systemic Approach—Classical Brief Strategic Model (*Seeks to answer the question, How is this a problem and what is maintaining it? Focuses on individual in context of relationships*)

Identified problem: Hierarchical incongruities within client's family system; eating disorder sustains balance within the family system.

Goal of therapy:	Explore organizational and interactional patterns within the family, particularly enmeshment, over-protectiveness, rigidity, lack of resolution, conflict, and triangulation.
Catalyst for change:	Strategic interventions.
Task of therapist:	Restructure family's organizational and interactional patterns and restore family to a more functional mode of operation.
Role of therapist:	Strategist.
Role of client:	Participant.

Third Wave: Systemic Approach—Mental Research Institute Model
(Seeks to answer the question, How is the problem being maintained and what is maintaining it?)

Identified problem:	Client's attempted solution to the complaint.
Goal of therapy:	Identify the complaint and the client's attempted solution in concrete and behavioral terms.
Catalyst for change:	Use of language; therapist maneuverability.
Task of therapist:	"Sell" the client on an intervention that is in opposition to her current solution pattern.
Role of therapist:	Strategist.
Role of client:	Participant.

The fourth wave is the solution-focused wave of clinical influence that delves into the development of solutions in therapy and looks to the existing resources and competencies inherent in the client as anchor points around which to formulate these solutions.

Fourth Wave: Solution-Focused Brief Therapy
(Seeks to answer the question, What needs to be different? Focuses on exceptions, that is, those times that the problem is not happening)

Identified problem:	Inability of client to recognize the absence of the problem.

Goal of therapy: Identify exceptions (either those times when binging, purging, or restricting is not problematic or other viable existing solution patterns) and help client repeat them.

Catalyst for change: Use of language, therapist expectancy, and key interventions based on client-therapist fit.

Task of therapist: Cooperate with client in identifying a salient goal, develop and build solutions, promote expectancy of change through use of language.

Role of therapist: Collaborator, student.

Role of client: Collaborator, active participant, expert in her own care.

Solution-Focused Brief Therapy

There can be little doubt that each wave has contributed significantly to the eating disorders field, both from the scientific and clinical standpoints. However, health care reform is launching clinicians into the fourth wave of influence. As the direct result of health care reforms, treatment providers, for the first time ever, are being held accountable for the clinical services they deliver and, if they are to compete, must demonstrate competency in cost-effective therapy that is measurable through clinical outcome studies.

This new launch, although generally not well received by the vast majority of clinicians, has in fact endowed the field with a significant gift. To become more efficient and clinically efficacious, therapists must shed the traditional treatment paradigm, which is pathology based and views clients as sick and defective, and replace it with the fourth wave paradigm, which is resource based and views clients as capable and competent in the management of their lives. Introducing the solution-focused model to a field that is anachronistically grappling with the causes of the disorders it treats and using cause-focused treatment approaches will be a challenge. A proliferation of clinical writings and investigations have dealt with eating disorders according to a medical model or a pathology-based paradigm in which causality is conceived to be linear and unidirectional (Johnson, 1991; Johnson & Brief 1983; Wooley & Kearney-Cooke 1986). Cognitive/behavioral approaches are gaining popularity due to positive outcome results. However, comparatively speaking, there has been a paucity of writings that address the treatment of eating disorders from a systemic theoretical model. (The major early contributors to the systemic model were mentioned in the discussion of the third wave.)

According to Steve deShazer (1991): "Where the structural view assumes that clients' problems are a reflection of a wrong or dysfunctional social organization and intervention is based on a map of what is supposedly a correct family hierarchy, the focused problem-solving model (MRI model) assumes that clients are doing the best they can and further assumes that family hierarchy or structure is not important in doing therapy. [The MRI model does not] assume a pathological, illness, or disease-oriented view of the family or family structure, but rather focus[es] on sequences of interaction and problem-solving behavior" (p. 55).

The Brief Family Therapy Center, founded by deShazer, also took the view that the client is doing the best she can but shifted from the MRI model by postulating that "if therapists accept the client's complaint as the reason for *starting* therapy, therapists should, by the same logic, accept the client's statement of satisfactory improvement as the reason for *terminating* therapy." From this postulate, "the idea developed that *the client's goals and solutions were more important than the problems the client depicted in the session*" [italics mine] (deShazer, 1991, p. 57).

Thus, the solution-focused model makes no assumptions about the "real" nature of the problem, takes the client at her word, and is interested in finding a solution that is salient and unique to that particular individual. Moreover, "assuming an atheoretical, non-normative, client determined posture toward . . . problems allows the mental health professional to relinquish the role of expert or teacher in favor of the role of student or apprentice. As such, the therapist serves the client by learning his unique way of conceptualizing the complaint that brings him into treatment" (Berg & Miller, 1992, p. 7).

Central to the solution-focused approach is the hypothesis that there are periods of time when the problem does *not* occur. These periods are called exceptions. As deShazer says, "Problems are seen to maintain themselves simply because they maintain themselves and because clients depict the problem as *always happening* [italics mine]. Therefore, times when the complaint is absent are dismissed as trivial by the client or even remain completely unseen, hidden from the client's view. Nothing is actually hidden, but although these exceptions are open to view, they are not seen by the client as differences that make a difference" (deShazer, 1991, p. 53).

In this model, the therapeutic interview consists of questions that orient the client toward exceptions and solutions by systematically encouraging her to imaginatively project herself into a future situation in which her problem is no longer present. The specific interviewing technique used to achieve this projection into a trouble-free future is the miracle question (explored in greater detail in Chapters Four and Seven), which asks the client to imagine that a miracle has occurred and she no longer has her problem at all. "Solution-determined conversations help clients describe and orient their lives in new ways," deShazer says (1991, p. 124), and the focus of therapy becomes "language games" that address three interrelated activities.

- Generating exceptions
- Picturing a new life for the client
- Validating that change is happening and that, in fact, the new life has already started

This model is also goal driven; consequently, the therapist and client work together in forming realistic and achievable treatment goals that are highly specific. Goals emerge from the miracle question or other solution-oriented interview questions, such as, What do you want to see different as a result of coming here? or, How will we know when therapy is finished? DeShazer (1990) finds that "in order for therapy to be brief and effective, both therapist and client need to know where they are going and they need to know how to know when they get there. . . . Most simply, a picture of 'life after successful therapy' can guide the work of both therapist and client" (p. 97).

The central philosophy of the solution-focused model involves three simple rules (Berg & Miller, 1992; Miller, 1992b):

1. If it ain't broke, *don't fix it*. The therapist should be concerned only with what the client is actively presenting as the problem, regardless of what the therapist may believe to be the problem and no matter how obvious the problem the therapist believes she or he sees.

2. Once you know what works, *do more of it*. When the therapist and the client discover a meaningful exception to the problem, a time or times when the problem is *not* happening, then a solution has probably been discovered and the client needs to do more of it.

3. If it doesn't work, then don't do it again; *do something different!* If something does not work, it is to be rigorously avoided by the therapist. As deShazer says, "Just about anything that is different stands a chance of making a difference" (deShazer, 1990, p. 94).

Developing and constructing solutions (rather than exploring causes and problems or examining the maintenance of problems within interactional patterns), offers clinicians a new therapeutic map. Although speculating about the causes of anorexia and bulimia is intellectually stimulating and an important area of research, it serves no immediate useful purpose in the *implementation* of solution-focused brief therapy. The major thrust of this therapy deals with what is problematic for the client *now* and what needs to happen so that the situation can improve. Moreover, although essential for pathology-based paradigms, risk factors in solution-focused brief therapy are of no consequence to the treatment process and result in therapeutic detours that promote wastefulness in treatment and actually clutter the therapeutic relationship. Rather than reexamining and dwelling on the past, solution-focused treatment focuses on the present and future. What difference does the client wish to see in her life *today?* What needs to happen so that she can get on with her life in a way that is meaningful to her?

Solution-focused brief therapy also dispenses with diagnostic labels. Although diagnostic definitions are important for scientific clarity, they are a major obstacle in the day-to-day practice of solution-focused treatment. Labeling predisposes the therapist to a particular set of assumptions about what's "wrong" with the client and encourages treatment that imposes the therapist's beliefs about "healthy functioning" on the client. As will be discussed in greater detail in Chapter Three, the solution-focused model refrains from using diagnostic labels or categorizing clients on the basis of symptoms. Lengthy clinical assessments that focus on problems, symptoms, and pathology are avoided. Taking time to determine whether someone meets specific diagnostic criteria not only interferes with the intensity and flow of solution-focused brief therapy but can also impair the quality of the therapeutic relationship.

Clinicians need to discover the client's specific complaint related to her dietary or binging and purging behaviors. Rather than pigeonholing the client, it is far more clinically efficacious to concentrate on the client's unique solution patterns for her problem behaviors. It is more respectful to view her simply as a "client" who has a complaint related to dietary practices rather than as an

"anorexic" or "bulimic." Clinical assessments that focus on establishing a diagnosis, the antecedents that may have played a causal
role in the disorder, the premorbid severity of the symptoms, the
client's eating and dieting history, and the possible occurrence of
an affective illness and Axis II diagnosis keep clinicians, and consequently clients, steeped in a morass of problems and symptoms,
all of which promote great inefficiency in the therapeutic process.
Not only are the client's goals for seeking treatment often eclipsed
when the therapist focuses on symptoms and history but the traditional diagnostic process can lock the client into the role of being
"sick" and have adverse effects on her self-esteem. At times, professionals from various disciplines have carelessly classified individuals as bulimic or anorexic and, in so doing, have actually
validated and consolidated a clinically labelled identity within these
persons, making treatment all the more complicated and inefficient.
Although documentation required by outside agencies still calls for
some of this diagnostic activity, as managed care continues to influence the course of clinical treatment the norms for documentation
will be affected and, in time, will reflect solution-based brief therapy principles. (I have already consulted with several managed care
groups and mental health agencies to redesign diagnostic assessment forms and treatment plans to be more reflective of solution-
oriented brief therapy tenets.)

In solution-focused therapy, treatment begins by delving immediately into the discovery of solutions. The client's presenting problem is simply taken at face value, as are her complaints regarding
her eating and dieting behaviors. Consequently, treatment is highly
individualized. Rather than treating an anorexic, bulimic, restricter,
purger, or bulimic-anorexic, the solution-focused brief therapist
treats the cluster of eating and/or dieting behaviors that the client
identifies as problematic. The clinician's role is to learn the client's
unique view of her problem and what needs to be different as a
result of treatment. As Milton Erickson says, "Each person is a
unique individual. Hence psychotherapy should be formulated to

meet the uniqueness of the individual's needs rather than tailoring the person to fit the Procrustean bed of a hypothetical theory of human behavior" (Berg & Miller, 1992, p. 8).

In order to comfortably discard diagnostic labels, however, clinicians must take the first step in becoming a solution-focused brief therapist. They must embrace the paradigm shift that requires them to view clients as inherently resourceful, basically healthy, and capable of solving their own problems. Thus, instead of operating from a deficit perspective in which the client is viewed as sick and broken, the clinician will operate from a resource perspective, assuming that the client is doing the best she can and is fully capable of resolving her specific complaint, that is, the complaint *she brings* to the therapist.

The solution-focused model maintains the premise that *nothing always happens*. There are always exceptions or nonproblem patterns, and the therapeutic task becomes one of assisting clients to discover these exceptions. In this view, the solutions are already within the client's existing repertoire of behaviors and, thus, likely to be repeatable. The therapist helps the client find ways of repeating the solution pattern, even under adverse situations. If this does not lead toward the client's goal, then the therapist must switch to tasks that require the client to do something differently. In this therapy, the client cooperation required is readily developed and promoted, since the therapist has concentrated right from the start on what the client is already doing that works for her.

In contrast to strategic family therapy, which requires that all members of the family be present for treatment, the solution-focused therapist treats the client-identified problem, regardless of the client's family status. As deShazer and Berg (1985) put it, "A problem is a problem; the number of people (and their relationship to one another) whom the therapist sees to help solve the problem does not seem a useful distinction. This of course presupposes a strong belief in the systemic concept of holism: If you change one element in a system . . . the system as a whole will be affected" (p. 97).

This solution-oriented approach is particularly empowering to the client. Eating disorder clients generally are steeped in pervasive feelings of shame, inadequacy, and personal impotency. They have spent a vast amount of energy trying to figure out the why of their perplexing behavior patterns. As they become preoccupied with food and weight and compile a highly developed nutritional knowledge base, they can easily become experts in their own inner dynamics. However, this expertise often only reinforces their overwhelming (and impossible) goal of achieving perfection.

In addition, partly because the physiological effects of dieting make their goal of "thinness" all the more elusive, eating disorder clients are particularly steeped in problem behaviors focused on food, calorie counting, and purging. The solution-focused approach jars them out of this obsessive cycle and into examining those times when their binge/purge behaviors are manageable or nonproblematic, thus greatly increasing their perceptions of self-efficacy. These exceptions, or "mastery experiences" as Bandura (1977, p. 196) calls them in discussing self-efficacy theory, are meaningful to the client since they are already a part of her existing behavior patterns.

Interrelation of Self-Efficacy, Self-Esteem, and Exceptions

Any clinician would be hard-pressed not to be keenly aware of the eating disorder client's pervasive feelings of inadequacy, powerlessness, and worthlessness. The client's level of self-esteem is intricately connected to both her perceptions of her *inner self* (feelings of competency and control) and her *outer self* (body image). As long as she can control her eating behaviors and maintain her body or weight within her ideal range, she reports feeling a greater sense of self-worth and control. Being in control, as reflected in her dietary regimen and weight, generally colors her outlook on the rest of her life in a very favorable way. Conversely, being out of control, as reflected in binging and purging behaviors and weight gain, spirals her into an abyss of despair and misery.

Because eating disorder clients typically suffer from cognitive distortions (Garner, 1986), they have a propensity for focusing on their inability to control themselves (self-inefficacy), particularly in relation to dieting and weight loss, *regardless of periods of abstinence*. Their tendency toward dichotomous thinking and perfectionism prevents them from being aware of contexts as well as from recognizing any small steps of success in achieving their desired goal (control as reflected in their weight). This lack of awareness, in turn, promotes a sense of powerlessness, which has deleterious effects on the client's overall level of self-esteem. As the client's self-esteem deteriorates, she isolates more and more, withdrawing into herself, turning to food or starvation for comfort, thus perpetuating the spiral of despair.

Unlike traditional therapy which attempts to reconstruct a competent, capable "self," solution-focused therapy starts at a much more basic level in addressing this critical issue of the competent self. DeShazer believes that individuals who have tried repeatedly to solve their problems with no success generally develop an evaluation of themselves as persons with an *insolvable complaint*. Furthermore, they establish deeply entrenched expectations for continued failure (deShazer, 1985). Not only are clients thinking it is "the same damn thing over and over again" (p. 75), but they are also thinking, "I don't have what it takes to control my binging and purging." The solution-focused model emphasizes the effects of insolvability on expectations of continued failure, rather than the effect of insolvability on the individual's level of self-efficacy.

For eating disorder clients, the issue of self-efficacy and self-esteem is particularly critical. The ability to be in control as reflected in their dieting and eating behaviors is a measure of their self-worth. These clients have repeatedly attempted to control their eating behaviors only to discover that the problem seems insolvable. They then take this insolvability to a much deeper level and view it as a personal deficiency; thus augmenting their already existing feelings of inefficacy, powerlessness, and helplessness.

By the time many eating disorder clients enter therapy, they have repeatedly attempted to control their eating or purging activities to no avail. Generally, they view this control as the magic bullet that will bring them everlasting happiness in *every* area of their lives if they can achieve it. I contend that their evaluation of themselves as inefficacious is what needs to be altered via the therapeutic process. The solution-focused model can achieve this alteration. Focusing on what's already working promotes a sense of self-efficacy because the client is no longer looking *outside* herself for solutions but is empowered to examine her own unique resources. The overall goal is for the client and therapist to negotiate a solvable problem, and this goal is accomplished by focusing primarily on the observable, that is, what can be described in clear and concrete terms.

Seeing Beyond the Mirror

As Brumberg (1988) has astutely noted, during the nineteenth century the scientific community was so preoccupied with authenticating symptoms and delineating diagnostic differentiations that no one thought simply to ask the patient known as the "fasting girl" her reason for choosing not to eat. Similarly today, etiology, diagnostic distinctions, and established standards of healthy individual and family functioning have taken precedence over simply asking the client about those times she is able to manage her problem behaviors and helping her make the "unrecognized difference become a difference that makes a difference" (deShazer, 1991, p. 10). Instead of focusing on the past, solution-focused brief therapy has a present and future orientation. The therapeutic process becomes a partnership between client and therapist in which every aspect of treatment is focused on solution development. The pattern of interaction between therapist and client is a critical factor in the model as, together, they explore the times the problem is not happening and makes these times the focus of treatment.

The fourth wave brings an entirely different clinical emphasis to the treatment of eating disorder clients. Perhaps it will be the sword that cuts the Gordian knot that has all too often confined researchers and clinicians in a negative mindset about these clients and their possibilities.

Three

Transforming Clinical Assumptions: Becoming Mindful

> "I can't believe *that!*" said Alice.
>
> "Can't you?" the Queen said in a pitying tone.
>
> "Try again: draw a long breath, and shut your eyes."
>
> —*Lewis Carroll*
> Through the Looking Glass

Before I was able to clinically practice solution-focused brief therapy with my individual clients and restructure the EDRC group program, I had to undergo a real shift in the assumptions I had been making for the past thirteen years about eating disorder clients and the clinical course of their treatment. This was not easy to do.

Bill O'Hanlon and Michele Weiner-Davis (1989) delineate the basic assumptions central to solution-oriented brief therapies in their book *In Search of Solutions*. These presuppositions, along with deShazer's similar principles (Berg & Miller, 1992), provided the foundation for my theoretical transition.

- Eating disorder clients have the necessary internal resources and competencies to surmount their own difficulties or solve their own problems.

- After eliciting the client's personal competencies, strengths, and resources, the therapist uses these characteristics to individualize the solution and lead the client to her desired goal.

- Client and therapist work together cooperatively, with the client functioning as the "expert" in her treatment and defining the goal of therapy.

- Change is viewed as inevitable and constant, and the therapeutic process is based on the belief that one small change in the system affects change in other parts of the system.

- Treatment focuses on what is possible and changeable. Knowing a great deal about the history and symptoms of eating disorders or focusing on "causes" is usually unnecessary.

- The therapist strives to be as economical as possible in obtaining desired therapeutic ends.

- Rapid change and healing is possible and meaningful.

- The therapist is an active participant in the process and her or his primary role is to identify, reinforce, and amplify change.

However, in order to accept these presuppositions, I had to let go of some strong, perhaps even rigid beliefs about the illnesses of anorexia and bulimia, the role of the therapist, the role of the "patient," and the therapeutic process itself. And I did not realize how tightly I clung to these beliefs until I had to relinquish them.

The gifted social psychologist Ellen Langer conducted fascinating research on the phenomenon of mindlessness and its inverse, mindfulness. According to Langer (1989), "When mindless, . . . people treat information as though it were context free—true regardless of circumstances" (p. 3). People become vulnerable to mindlessness when they cannot see beyond the categories they develop in order to manage phenomena. To exemplify this vulnerability, Langer tells how she became interested in studying mindless behaviors.

My grandmother complained to her doctors about a snake crawling around beneath her skull and giving her headaches. Her descriptions were vivid and figurative, not literal. That was just the way she talked. But the young doctors who took care of her paid little attention to what this very old lady from another culture was telling them. They diagnosed senility. Senility comes with old age, after all, and makes people talk nonsense. When she grew more confused and unhappy, they recommended electroconvulsive therapy and convinced my mother to give her approval.

Not until an autopsy was performed did anyone detect my grandmother's brain tumor. I shared my mother's agony and guilt. But who were we to question the doctors? [Langer, 1989, pp. 2–3].

The physicians, not open to what the patient was describing, made a diagnosis based on their mindset of senility, while Langer's family accepted this diagnosis based on their mindset about experts. Conversely, the three key qualities of a mindful state of being are willingness to create new categories, openness to new information, and awareness of more than one perspective.

In order to alter my clinical beliefs and habits so that I could adopt the assumptions of solution-focused therapy, I had to become more *mindful*, that is, open to an entirely new view of the psychotherapeutic process and the therapist's role in it. Today, as I refine my ability to be mindful with my clients, I keep my theories and previously established mindsets away from sessions, so that I do not take clients for granted. By abandoning labels of anorexic or bulimic, I am better able to be open to the uniqueness of the individual client. Interviewing for solution patterns and exceptions has heightened my awareness of and sensitivity to the resourcefulness and survivorship of those individuals who have complaints about their eating, their weight, or their relationship with food.

As human beings we are all susceptible to mindless behaviors, therefore a fuller description of my experiences as I transitioned from a pathologically focused to a solution-focused paradigm may be useful to other clinicians. The first step I took to liberate myself from the tyranny of my old mindsets about eating disorders was to modify my basic clinical assumptions about eating disorders and the therapeutic process in the direction of the solution-focused assumptions listed at the beginning of the chapter. In the following sections,

I describe the kinds of changes I had to make to achieve each new assumption.

ASSUMPTION: *Eating disorder clients have the necessary internal resources and competencies to surmount their own difficulties or solve their own problems.*

Anorexia nervosa and bulimia nervosa are diagnoses that have become pejorative labels signifying hard-to-treat clients who have serious psychopathology. Indeed, in my experience, eating disorder clients are viewed by most clinicians and referral sources as *notoriously* difficult to treat. For most clinicians, anorexia conjures up an image of a extremely willful, uncooperative, emaciated individual who cannot be taken at her word; bulimia calls to mind an individual who is secretive about her relationship with food, manipulative, overcompliant, and ambivalent about recovery.

These clients are characterized as seeking perfection, being achievement oriented, and suffering from repressed affect, particularly anger. Their families are viewed as rigid and enmeshed, suffering from dysfunctional communication and relationship patterns: "Compared to other families, the families of bulimics have been found to be less caring, less cohesive, and more overprotective and to have higher levels of conflict and hostility" than other families (Kent & Clopton, 1992, p. 281).

To further complicate the clinical profile, in recent years, evidence has accumulated of the high levels of co-morbidity of anorexia and bulimia with affective, anxiety, substance abuse, and personality disorders (Herzog et al., 1992): "Depending on samples and diagnostic criteria used, formal personality disorders are reported to be present in 50 to 75 percent of cases [of patients who are both anorexic and bulimic] with 14 to 40 percent displaying co-morbid borderline personality disorder" (Steiger, Leung, & Freedom, 1993, p. 47).

Such findings reinforce the perception that eating disorder clients are difficult to treat and require long-term therapy to effect characterological changes, and a similar mindset about characterological deficits blocked my ability to be open to the possibility that the client had any patterns of health within her repertoire of behaviors or family/support system. I believed eating disorder clients to be deeply wounded, emotionally unstable individuals who came from severely dysfunctional family systems. After thirteen years of treating these clients, I would unconsciously "categorize" them according to their reported symptoms and pathological behavior patterns. Although I recognized the complexity of the illness and experienced a continuum of clients, my mindset precluded me from exploring the unique world of each one. I took my clients out of the context of their own experiences so that they could fit the label I ascribed to them.

Before I could see the resourcefulness of my clients, I had to suspend my diagnostic judgments and put my speculations away. My posture had to become that of the curious interviewer who asked numerous questions for not only a greater understanding of the client's world but also a knowledge of what she wanted to be different as a result of our time together. I had to achieve a state of being ever mindful of the client's resources, strengths, and competencies, before I could help her allow herself to be mindful of these qualities.

Erickson believed that the basic problem for mental health clients was not pathology or defect but rather their own rigidity. They have become stuck by failing to use a range of skills, competencies, and learnings that they possess but simply are not using (O'Hanlon, 1987). I discovered that the basic problem for me as a therapist was my own rigidity, which left me "stuck" along with the clients who felt frustrated by the tenacity of their illness or their denial. Being open to the resourcefulness of clients, as the following example illustrates, has exposed me to clinical resourcefulness in myself.

Case Study

A hospital-based inpatient program referred the "Sims" family to me for "ongoing, long-term family therapy." "Allie," the daughter, was an eighteen-year-old anorexic who had been hospitalized for two months and was now ready for discharge. The therapist who had treated her and her family described them as the "typical" anorexic family, in which the mother was uptight, dominant, and controlling, and the father was relatively passive and absent from the home due to heavy travel connected with work. She described the marital pair as highly dysfunctional with the mother covertly hostile toward the father and extremely emotionally distant from him. The father was viewed as uninvolved with the family and as a type A personality, "always working, never home." The therapist also said that Allie was extremely self-centered, highly manipulative, and demanded an incredible amount of attention and would do just about anything to get it. She wished me luck and added, "You're going to need it." (Many of my referral sources end their conversations with me in a similar vein.)

But when I interviewed the family to determine what changes had occurred as a result of Allie's two-month inpatient experience, I was flabbergasted. The parents reported significant changes in her eating patterns, her attitude about food, and her moods in general. Our entire first session was spent reviewing, amplifying, and reinforcing the dramatic changes this family had made.

Her father had completely altered his travel patterns so that he could participate in Allie's treatment. He agreed to continue to do this, so he could be available for these sessions. The parents reported that he and Allie had been interacting more and had actually begun to take weekly walks together. Allie had terminated what she described as a very dysfunctional, dependent relationship with her boyfriend of three years. Her mother described a very volatile family scene that had occurred the week before and how they were able to reach a resolution in an ongoing conflict over the use of the family car.

Even though Mrs. Sims's voice during the telling of this incident was often laced with hostility and her glances toward Mr. Sims could be interpreted as demeaning, I chose not to respond to these behaviors and instead explored in detail how the conflict had been resolved and how this interaction was different from previous ones. A few times when Allie was not involved in the session discussion, she would physically curl up on the couch and write in her notebook. Once again, I chose not to attend to these behaviors but instead enlarged upon the changes the family described.

As I listened to their stories of change, I was extremely struck by the concern these parents had for their daughter and for their family as a whole. It was very clear to me that they had put a tremendous amount of effort into making things better. They were listening to each other more, communicating more openly, and the father was making himself more available both emotionally and physically. At the end of the first session, I complimented all three of them profusely for the dramatic changes they had made and told them to keep doing more of the same! This family continued to make gains in therapy after nine sessions that lasted over a five-month period.

The Sims family illustrates a key point. An anorexic family can have strengths, resources, and functional patterns of communication as long as therapists look for them and amplify them in the treatment process. Conversely, mindsets that look only for pathology can easily undermine the family or the individual's capacity for self-healing and self-regulation.

Research has demonstrated that teacher expectations have a powerful effect on students' behavior (Rosenthal & Jacobsen, 1968). Similarly, therapist expectations can have a major impact on clients' behavior (Watzlawick, 1984). The issue of therapist expectancy will be explored further in the next chapter. But the old adage "What you look for is what you get" succinctly describes a major belief of the solution-focused approach.

ASSUMPTION: *After eliciting the client's personal competencies, strengths, and resources, the therapist uses these characteristics to individualize the solution and lead the client to her desired goal.*

Brief therapists use whatever the client brings to the session as a potential therapeutic key to unlocking the problem. Therefore, the clinician must work within the client's frame of reference, even though eating disorder clients can hold some very unusual beliefs, behaviors, or idiosyncrasies. These peculiarities are often viewed by the therapist as just that . . . unusual and a part of the illness. In becoming mindful, I had to make a 180-degree turn before I could use these unusual aspects in developing salient solutions.

When I first specifically began exploring the client's resources and solution patterns, I was not only skeptical of their effectiveness but in many cases concerned about their medical and psychological consequences. The change in technique required great faith on my part.

Case Study

I received a call from a mother requesting an appointment for her eighteen-year-old anorexic daughter, "Zed." The family was seeking treatment at this time because Zed's counselor recommended that she withdraw from her university to get more intensive therapy.

When the mother called for the appointment, she indicated that Zed already had been seen by their family physician and her labs were borderline. She wanted to know who should come in for the appointment. I told her I felt that was a family decision and I would see whoever wanted to be involved. This was a real departure from my usual protocol which required that the entire family be present.

Zed and both of her parents arrived for the first appointment. Zed was an attractive, pleasant young woman. She was somewhat verbal and initially expressed that things were better since she had returned home from school. She reported that she was trying to eat but quickly added that this was extremely difficult for her, especially since she would feel uncomfortably full after any of these attempts.

Zed had seen a counselor at the university for the past four months and said this had been helpful. She said she wanted to be "normal" again. When we explored what this meant for her, she identified two signs of normalcy for herself: one, she would be calling her friends on the phone and going out with them instead of hanging out in her bedroom, and two, she would be eating more as she used to, when it had not been such an effort. When asked how she had been able to eat at all since her return home, she said it was not easy. Her dad said they never saw her eat and were really worried about her. He also said they had a long-standing family rule that they all have dinner together; however, dinnertime had been a disaster for them since Zed returned from school.

Her mother commented that, although she was glad Zed was actually sitting down at the table with them, it was an extremely stressful time, since Zed would want to know every ingredient of every dish and then would then recite the calorie count or fat grams of each item. This recitation would incense the father since he saw how much it upset the mother, Zed would complain bitterly about what her mother had prepared, and mealtime always ended in a major blowup with Zed crying, storming off from the table, and then locking herself in her bedroom for the remainder of the evening.

During our session, Zed finally blurted out, "I don't know why you won't let me cook. When I was on campus at the apartment, I cooked all of the time." I asked, "How was your eating different then?" She thought for a moment and said, "Well, now that you ask, I wouldn't sit down with my roommates, but I would nibble here and there as I was cooking. I had control of the entire kitchen." Her mother, however, was adamant that she did not want Zed cooking, since she felt that was her responsibility. Her father agreed and felt that Zed should be doing fun things: "There'll be plenty of time for you to be cooking. So don't rush it." Once again, Zed brought up the fact that she really loved concocting meals for her roommates and that she was considered by them to be an excellent gourmet cook. While on campus, she had taken cooking lessons at a department store near the university and joined a gourmet cooking club, and she had actually catered a few fraternity parties. Zed was quite animated as she talked about these experiences.

I asked if the family would be willing to try something different that would require hard work on everybody's part. They agreed to try what was suggested. Zed and her mother were to plan one dinner together, and Zed was to shop for the ingredients. While Zed was preparing the meal, her mother was to sit at the kitchen table and write the nutritional content of each dish on a 3 x 5 card. The card was to include calories, fat content, cholesterol content, and any other nutritional information she and Zed deemed important. She was to place these information cards next to Zed's plate. Zed was to agree to telephone at least one friend after dinner was over and tell her father she had completed the call.

The family returned a week later and reported that things were much better. The assignment was so successful that Zed and her mother ended up preparing four meals together. Her father reported that Zed ate something at every meal, and he felt less worried. There was less fighting at the table, so Zed spent less time in her room and had reconnected with an old high school chum via the phone.

In this case, Zed's pleasure and interest in cooking as well as her need to know the nutritional details of what she ate became part of the solution. Her mother's kitchen responsibility was temporarily shifted from cooking to detailing nutrients, which still left her in the kitchen at mealtime. Her father felt less worried since he saw Zed eating something and felt that she at least was taking a step in the right direction toward increasing her social activity. And the dinnertime fighting stopped.

Another case also illustrates the effectiveness of using the client's resources.

Case Study

A physician referred "Kellee," a fourteen-year-old anorexic to the Eating Disorders Recovery Center (EDRC), describing her as "a very sick youngster" and her family as "the most disturbed, dysfunctional family" he had ever been involved with. He reported that she was bordering on her acceptable weight level of ninety pounds and that her hospitalized weight would be eighty-nine pounds. He briefed me regarding Kellee's history, which included two hospitalizations and numerous attempts at outpatient therapy. The parents had had great difficulty following through with outpatient treatment and had complaints about every therapist they saw. His last words to me were, "Good luck with this case. They will no doubt be the most difficult family you have ever worked with."

At our first session, which included Kellee, her seventeen-year-old sister, "Angie," and both parents, no one was really clear why the family was there. Kellee did not think there was a special problem at all, since all families have problems, and both she and Angie thought therapy was a waste of time since their other attempts at therapy never really seemed to make a difference. They both agreed that they were tired of starting over with yet another therapist and having to repeat the same old information again. The father complained about the previous psychiatrist who seemed to blame him and his wife for Kellee's anorexia, and the mother just wanted the family to communicate better.

Both Kellee and Angie did not want family therapy, and the parents did not disagree with their daughters. It was clear that Angie demonstrated leadership in the family and was the one to whom the parents always deferred. I must admit that during this session the words of the physician echoed repeatedly in my head—"disturbed and dysfunctional." My usual approach was simply not working with this family. For the first time, the miracle question about what they would like to see that was different fell flat and ended in refusal on everyone's part to participate. I felt that the session was disjointed and going nowhere, so recovering as best I could, I terminated it. After much thought and reviewing the videotape time and time again, I decided to write the family a letter summarizing the session and complimenting both Kellee and Angie for the very close relationship I had observed between them (actually Angie appeared to be the most functional family member, and she had been Kellee's key source of support, even during the hospitalizations). I also complimented the parents for their concern for their family as evidenced by their numerous attempts at treatment. Then I made two recommendations: first, that the parents think about what difference they would like to see as a result of counseling and then call me for an appointment, and second, that either of the girls could contact me if they wished to have counseling. These recommendations were based on one condition: Kellee would continue to see her pediatrician for weigh-ins and maintain her weight of ninety pounds. The mother called me two days after receipt of the letter to make an appointment for herself and her husband. She said they all liked the idea that the girls could decide on their own to come in but emphasized that the girls would have to come in together, since Kellee would never come in without Angie. I agreed.

I met with the parents a few times and attempted to identify a workable goal for counseling. During the course of these sessions, the referring physician called to say that Kellee's weight was dropping and he was on the verge of hospitalizing her. On the same day, the mother called to tell me that the girls wanted to come in and see me; she also confirmed that Kellee was not doing well.

When I met with the girls, Angie said she was worried about Kellee now that her weight had dropped again. The three of us identified a goal to work on: keep Kellee out of the hospital. Subsequent sessions focused on the exceptions, that is, the times Kellee was able to get her weight as high as ninety-five pounds, in order to use the same steps to keep her out of the hospital. The girls came in together for these sessions and did not want their parents involved. I agreed. During this time, I was able to use Angie as a means of highlighting, amplifying, and reinforcing changes Kellee was making. This was particularly useful because, initially, Kellee did not view these changes as that "big of a deal." Working with the two of them together in stabilizing her weight proved to be extremely effective. Kellee slowly reached ninety-three pounds and, eventually, the girls agreed to participate in family sessions, but they initiated the idea.

Previously, I would have diagnosed Kellee and Angie's relationship as enmeshed and codependent, labelled Angie as the family hero, and attempted to shift the power base to the parents. I would have never agreed to treat only two members of the family (and siblings at that!) and not to treat the anorexic singularly and the family as a whole. An interesting footnote is that the referring physician called me to ask what kind of magic I was using with this family! He was amazed that they continued to work with me and that we were able not only to stabilize Kellee's weight but also to get her to gain three pounds. The magic was simply to make this particular family's greatest resource a launching point and then proceed from there.

In working with clients and families who have complaints related to eating, restricting, or purging behaviors, using their existing positive abilities often requires a leap of faith, but for me, that leap has repeatedly proven to be a "magical" ingredient in developing salient solutions.

ASSUMPTION: *Client and therapist work together cooperatively, with the client functioning as the "expert" in her treatment and defining the goal of therapy.*

Like most treatment providers, I once believed that I was responsible for helping clients make the changes necessary not only to manage the symptoms of their eating disorder but also to learn about and manage their "addiction," deal with their guilt, understand the cultural implications of their illness, diminish their shame, and resolve the deficits related to their dysfunctional birth families. I was teaching clients to accept my beliefs about eating disorders and was exploring issues I thought relevant to recovery.

In solution-focused brief therapy, I had to set aside this approach and work on finding ways to join with the client in a collaboration. Steve Gilligan (1990, p. 362) refers to this process as "co-creating realities" and uses the metaphor of running a three-legged race to illustrate its value. As long as each partner is working with the other, they are able to progress toward the finish line, but when they are out of sync, *both* fall down and lose.

Instead of working "on" the client in a hierarchical relationship in which the therapist is viewed as "superior," the brief therapist, like the homeopathic healer, works "with" the client in a cooperative, egalitarian, mutually influencing partnership. The therapist cannot separate herself or himself from the therapeutic process and consequently is positioned "within" rather than "outside" the system (Hoffman, 1985).

According to deShazer (1984), in this cooperative view there is no such thing as "resistance." In traditional therapy, clients are viewed as resistant when they do not comply with the treatment regimen or the therapist's directives, and the resistance of eating disorder clients is legendary. As Vitousek, Daly, and Heiser (1991, p. 649) put it in summarizing the research of numerous investigators who have identified subtypes of denial in eating disorder patients, "Individuals with eating disorders may deny or distort specific behaviors (such as vomiting, laxative abuse, and dietary rituals); affective states and beliefs; the objective size and shape of their bodies; the characterization of their attitudes and behaviors as irrational, pathological or dangerous; and the attribution of their symptoms to particular causal factors." Moreover, these individuals are "disposed to deny anything and everything . . . even their own denial"!

Such extensive identification of denial presupposes an adversarial relationship between therapist and client. Entering the therapeutic relationship with this kind of belief about the client sets up a win/lose dynamic in which the therapist attempts to control the relationship only to lose control in the end. But instead of recognizing that we clinicians have lost, which is evidenced by treatment drop-out or blatant noncompliance (usually labelled resistance), we tend to blame the client for being uncooperative and difficult or the "disease" for being too entrenched and chronic. We rarely look at ourselves as a major element in the equation. DeShazer suggests that resistance is "redescribed" when the therapist operates within the therapeutic system. In this model, cooperation is assumed, since it is believed that the client is doing the very best she can. Consequently, what she reports is accepted at face value. The solution-focused therapist strives to accept the individual's view of the world and work *within* that frame of reference in order to facilitate the change process. A natural outcome of such an approach is a deeply respectful relationship.

The solution-focused brief therapist, in working *with* the eating disorder client, can establish goals that are meaningful, realistic, and achievable *to that client*. In my clinical experience, when I work cooperatively with clients, letting them choose their course of treatment as well as developing their treatment goals, treatment proceeds smoothly and much more efficiently. Also, as I work more cooperatively with clients, I recognize that some clients are able to make changes on their own and direct their own change, and my job becomes one of reinforcing those changes, rather than directing them according to my view of what needs to be changed.

The concepts of cooperation and co-creating realities were, at first, particularly elusive ones for me, especially given the role physiology plays in the eating disorders. The interplay between physiology and behavior cannot be ignored, particularly with the severely medically compromised anorexic client. In my experience, which is supported by the literature (Yates, 1990), it is extremely difficult to establish a psychotherapeutic relationship while the patient is severely malnourished. Starvation has been shown to alter mood, cognitive ability, and character traits (Yates, 1992). When in a starved state, anorexic patients are often described as moody, withdrawn, depressed, hostile, controlling, and obsessed with calorie counting or exercise. Indeed, starvation itself, can "cause the eating disorder to become entrenched and resistant to treatment" (Yates, 1992, p. 744).

Thus, the first and most difficult step in treating any anorexic is to facilitate physiological stabilization. The solution-focused model offers a unique approach to this potential battleground for control. Anorexics have a morbid fear of gaining weight and will do anything to prevent this from happening. Concurrently, however, they have equally adverse feelings regarding hospitalization. Rather than focus on weight gain and food plans, it is much more effective to join with the client in her desire to stay out of the hospital.

In Kellee's case, for example, she and I and Angie never identified weight gain as the goal of therapy but rather concentrated on what would have to happen so that she could avoid hospitalization, stop going to the pediatrician's office for weigh-ins, and stop coming to therapy. Thus, subgoals related to eating and weight came directly from the client in her desire to achieve the main goals she identified as salient to her. For instance, she identified "being carefree" as a goal that would help prevent hospitalization. When we explored how she was different when she was being carefree, she identified asking her sister out for lunch and then actually eating a half of a sandwich in front of her sister as a sign of being carefree. This was a clear and concrete goal (which involved eating) established by the client and one that she was more likely to accomplish than a direct goal of weight gain.

Once the client has achieved her goal of avoiding hospitalization, therapy can encourage the changes that are making this goal possible. In Kellee's case, once she stabilized her weight, we then began identifying what had to be different so that she could terminate therapy.

The next case study also illustrates the importance of cooperating with the client.

Case Study

Mr. "Milan" called the EDRC requesting counseling for his fifteen-year-old daughter, "Rae," who had an eating disorder. He wanted to set up an appointment for her, but wanted me to meet with his wife first, so she could review Rae's treatment history. In a rushed tone, he went on to briefly describe all the therapy his daughter and the entire family had received in the past three years. When I asked if anything was better or different since the onset of treatment, he said, now in an exasperated tone, that nothing was any better and that his daughter had a lot of serious problems. When I suggested that his wife bring Rae in for the first appointment, he repeated, only more emphatically, that he wanted his wife there at the first session and then his daughter would follow for the next appointment. I agreed to his plan and set up the appointment.

According to Mrs. Milan's first session review of Rae's previous treatment, Rae had begun self-mutilating when she was twelve (her mother recalled two specific incidents) and around the same time started to restrict her eating. She engaged in highly ritualistic eating patterns, which her mother described as extremely bizarre and disruptive to the family. The family sought treatment with a psychiatrist, who treated Rae individually and the family in family therapy. Rae reported to her mom that she did not like going to therapy and that it was a waste of her parents' money and her time. Her weight continued to drop, at which time she was hospitalized and medically stabilized. Mrs. Milan reported that she and her husband were becoming increasingly uncomfortable with this psychiatrist, since Mrs. Milan felt blamed for her daughter's problems. After a year and a half with him, they decided to seek treatment elsewhere.

The therapist they went to next, considered an expert in eating disorders, recommended that Rae have group therapy with her, individual therapy with her associate, and that all the family members participate in family therapy. Once again, Rae protested and said she did not want to go. The Milans insisted that she follow the treatment regimen prescribed. During this time, Rae's eating continued to be highly ritualistic. However, for the past year and a half, Rae had been going to therapy three times a week and the family once a week. Just a few weeks ago, Mrs. Milan reported, Rae had a flashback of being sexually abused when she was four or five years of age by a neighbor. However, Mr. Milan's medical insurance company had changed, and this particular therapist was not on the new company's provider list, a situation that resulted in the family's phone call to EDRC.

Rae's previous therapist had recommended that she needed long-term therapy to work through her recent revelation. When I asked if Rae agreed with this recommendation, Mrs. Milan said no; in fact, Rae did not want to see anybody anymore, and she did not want to talk about this flashback, and nobody could make her.

After Mrs. Milan was satisfied that I had enough background information about her daughter, I asked what was better since the family started all the therapy. She was somewhat startled by the question and said, "No one has ever asked me that before." But after some thought, she reported some dramatic changes not only in regard to Rae's eating disorder but also in terms of how the parents negotiated with Rae. Rae had not had any further self-mutilation incidents; she had also been eating somewhat more normally and had dramatically altered her ritualistic eating and cooking patterns. Although she had never been very social, she had recently become involved in a dance group and had started to take singing lessons. Her weight had normalized, and her menstrual cycle had resumed. She was, however, exercising frenetically two to three hours a day.

After I explored and amplified all of the things that had changed since the family began therapy, Mrs. Milan asked, "When does anyone ever know when they are finished with therapy?" I asked her if she felt she was finished with therapy. She thought for a long time and said, "I agree with Rae. I don't think we need any more therapy right now, but maybe later. Maybe you could just see her once, just so she could get to meet you and then if she someday felt like she needed to talk more—about this flashback—maybe then she could call you. Is that all right?" I complimented Mrs. Milan for all the hard work she had done in trying to help her daughter and agreed with her that perhaps it was best that they take a break from therapy and concentrate on using all the skills they had learned during the last three years.

Mrs. Milan still wanted me to meet with her daughter, and the interview with Rae supported the changes that Mrs. Milan had identified. Rae did not want to talk about her flashback at this time and felt that she had had enough therapy for now. I reviewed what she was currently doing that was working for her, and she reported that she felt confident that she could continue to maintain these changes. Treatment was terminated with the idea that Rae could return when she felt she needed more therapy.

Six weeks later, Mr. Milan called the center to set up an appointment for Rae. This time, it was Rae's idea.

It is often assumed that the eating disorder client and her family are not only limited in their ability to decide what is in their own best interests but also in their resiliency or resourcefulness. However, being mindful and respectful of their considerable capabilities promotes a high level of cooperation.

ASSUMPTION: *Change is viewed as inevitable and constant, and the therapeutic process is based on the belief that one small change in the system affects change in other parts of the system.*

The solution-focused therapist looks for those times when the problem is not a problem. In traditional therapy, binge-purge patterns are often discussed in excruciating detail by client and therapist to identify the precipitating cues for the behavior. Different results are obtained when the therapist focuses on the exceptions, those times the client is *not* binging, purging, or restricting and those times the client is able to do something different when the urge to binge, purge, or restrict occurs.

Focusing on the problem presupposes that the problem is constant and always lacks change. Focusing on the exceptions dispels the belief that the problem *always* happens. Eating disorder clients are rigidly focused on their eating, restricting, or purging behaviors and are eager to talk about them as they try to figure out how to control them. Orienting these clients toward exceptions instead helps them be mindful of change and promotes a sense of hopefulness. The solution-focused model shifts the client from asking, "Why do I do this?" to examining, "When I *don't* do this." As the client examines those times when there is no problem, the therapist assists her to focus on the details of what is different about those exceptional times.

Not only is change constant, but it has a ripple, or domino, effect. Change is contagious and follow-up studies at the Brief Family Therapy Center (BFTC) and the Mental Research Institute seem to empirically support this hypothesis. One follow-up question asks former clients, "Have any old problems that were not directly dealt with in therapy improved since you finished therapy at BFTC?" In one study, fifteen of twenty-three clients surveyed reported improvement in some of these "old problems" (deShazer, 1985). Our follow-up studies reveal similar results (see Chapter One). Believing as I now do that even small changes are generative of further changes means that I also believe that successful change increases the client's confidence level in her ability to solve other more difficult problems. The case of Zed is a good example of the ripple effect—a change that took advantage of her cooking interests generated a series of other changes, both within the family and within Zed herself.

Many eating disorder programs or treatment regimens identify major physical, interpersonal, and intrapsychic changes as treatment goals. Clients are referred to our center for "long-term therapy" to work through and resolve not only the eating disorder itself but "issues" related to the eating disorder. These issues range in scope from major depression to anxiety attacks, sexual abuse, substance abuse, spending abuse, kleptomania, and unresolved mother-daughter conflicts.

With so many goals to contend with, it is a wonder more clients do not ask Mrs. Milan's question: When do people know they are finished with therapy?

ASSUMPTION: *Treatment focuses on what is possible and changeable. Knowing a great deal about the complaint or focusing on "causes" is usually unnecessary.*

Erickson did not believe that it was necessary to know the cause of a symptom or problem in order to achieve resolution. "Etiology is a complex matter and not always relevant to getting over a problem" (O'Hanlon & Wilk [quoting Erickson], 1987, p. 17). When EDRC was first opened, I and the other therapists took an extensive history of each client. Our assessment consisted of an eating disorders questionnaire, a family assessment, a psycho-social history, an eating disorders history, drug and alcohol assessment, and body image assessment. A therapist would often spend one or two sessions in individual treatment detailing the client's history. As a result, clients spent considerable time talking about their binging and purging, their shame and guilt, their lack of assertiveness, their anger, or their relationships with their mothers. Obsessing over the why of their eating and searching for causes kept them in the morass of their pain.

Since EDRC is licensed by the Ohio Department of Mental Health, we are still required by that agency to gather certain historical clinical data. However, we have developed a self-report assessment form (see Resource A) that the client completes along with her general registration forms at her first appointment just prior to her first session. This procedure allows us to begin solution-focused therapy in the very first contact with the client. In this solution-focused therapy, we attend to the nondominant side of clients who view themselves as inadequate, shameful, and defective, and who want to understand their problem so they can control it. As the therapist helps the client look to a future in which she can get beyond her rigid mindset to the discovery of salient solutions, the therapist also promotes a real sense of client hopefulness about life ahead.

I have discovered that having too much information promotes mindlessness. I am more likely to regress to categorizing and labeling when I get too much background information or spend too much time on the problem. Conversely, when I attend to solution patterns and co-create with my clients, our mindfulness expands together.

Case Study

"Lani," a twenty-six-year-old professional woman, was referred by a local employee assistance program for "long-term therapy." The referring counselor reported that Lani was a "hard-core anorexic as an adolescent." She had been hospitalized and been given several years of outpatient therapy in her hometown. She was seeking treatment at this time because she was starting to be very restrictive in her eating. When Lani came to see me, she mentioned that she had been hospitalized for two months ten years ago for anorexia nervosa and had been in outpatient group and individual psychotherapy for three and a half years. She also described how, after getting her MBA from a university in California, she had moved to Cincinnati where she had gotten a very competitive job. She was extremely upset that she was exhibiting anorexic-like symptoms since she thought she had her eating disorder under control.

After exploring exceptions, we found that her eating was more normal on the weekends when she visited friends and family in

Indianapolis. What was different about those weekends was that she felt more "connected." With her friends, she could really be herself and open up to them. As we discussed this further, she began to lament that she did not have any really close friends in Cincinnati and that she never imagined it would be so difficult to meet people and form relationships. Since she had nothing to do in the evenings, she found herself staying very late at work and coming home and dropping into bed from exhaustion.

As she talked about what was different in Indianapolis, she recognized that she was isolating herself in Cincinnati and had not made any serious attempts to "build a life here." She decided to enroll in a health club and leave work at a reasonable hour. At our second and last session, which took place three weeks after the first session at her request, Lani reported that things were much better. She had enrolled in a health club and was going there right after work. She said that she was not restricting as much and that she had met a young woman at the club who worked at the same company she did. She felt confident that she could get herself back on the right track.

Rather than exploring the causes for Lani's relapse, treatment focused on what was changeable and already working for her. The exception served as the actual solution to her problem.

ASSUMPTION: *The therapist strives to be as economical as possible in obtaining desired therapeutic ends.*

Steve deShazer prefers the simplest and most direct means to an end and this view is central to the solution-focused model (Miller, 1992b). The solution-focused brief therapist accepts the client's complaint at face value and then chooses the least invasive treatment strategy. As deShazer (1988) says, "From a minimalist's perspective, it is best to assume that a wet bed is simply a wet bed, teeth-grinding is teeth grinding, voices as voices and nothing more.

We have more complex explanatory metaphors available upon which to build a treatment approach should the first, most minimal approach fail" (p. 150).

This too is an approach I have adopted.

Case Study

"Catie," a thirty-two-year-old professional woman, was referred to me by an employee assistance counselor because of her bulimia and flashbacks to sexual abuse. When I asked her what brought her in, she hesitated before saying, "the other counselor said I needed to work on my eating disorder and resolve this thing with my dad. She felt the two were related and that until I resolved this abuse thing I would never get over the bulimia. She also said I will probably have more flashbacks." When I asked if she agreed with the counselor, she said, "Not really. I think I accepted this thing with my dad, and I know I could get my binging and purging under control if I could just figure out what to do about my two-year-old daughter."

After some discussion, Catie revealed that she had one memory of her dad fondling her when she was three or four. She had shared this with her husband early in their marriage and felt that she had come to terms with it. Now that they had a child of their own, he refused to let their daughter spend the night with Catie's parents or be with Catie's father unless Catie and her husband were both there. She said she felt terribly guilty about not letting her daughter go to her parents when the daughter was allowed to spend unsupervised time with Catie's husband's folks. Her dilemma was whether she should tell her mother or her father about this memory, so that they would understand why their grandchild was not allowed to be alone with them.

After we explored her options, Catie decided to write her mother a letter explaining what happened, and then give it to her in person at a time when they could talk about it further if her mother wanted to. Once she made this decision, she was able to report that her eating was back to normal, and therapy was terminated at the third session.

Follow-up at three months and six months indicated that Catie was maintaining control of her eating and that, although there was initial turmoil over the letter, things were beginning to settle down. At the six-month follow-up, Catie's mom and dad had just started to see their church minister, and she viewed this as extremely positive.

This case serves to illustrate that by working *with* the client, using a "bottom-up" approach and staying focused on *her* goal for treatment, she was able to solve her own problem and do so efficiently.

ASSUMPTION: *Rapid change and healing is possible and meaningful.*

Many clinicians hold firm to the belief that "more is better," and that it takes "more" to effect meaningful change in psychotherapy. However, the research on outcomes does not support this notion. In fact, it demonstrates that the major positive impact of individual psychotherapy occurs within the first six to eight sessions (Budman & Gurman, 1988). Solution-focused brief therapy is highly specific and goal driven. With specific and concrete client-determined goals as the bedrock for intervention, therapy is highly efficient; therefore, rapid change is inevitable.

When therapy emphasizes intervention tasks, clients are expected to work outside of therapy, which is where the "real" therapy takes place. In solution-focused brief therapy, clients are either observing or doing some other task between each and every session. Both factors—specific client-determined goals that emerge from the therapeutic relationship and homework tasks—promote therapeutic efficiency, which in turn creates rapid change.

Given all that has been written about the nature of eating disorders and the resistances and severe psychopathology of the sufferers and their families, one might feel safe in assuming that a complete psychological, physical, and interpersonal restoration could take a very long time and require various modalities including individual therapy, group therapy, family therapy, and nutritional therapy. However, when we clinicians operate from a resource perspective and work *with* the client and reinforce change, we communicate to the client that we expect change to occur and are sure it will happen. Our belief about change can dramatically affect the client's expectations of change and shorten expected length of treatment.

Case Study

"Ronnie," a thirty-two-year-old, sought treatment because she wanted to stop her binge-purge cycle. However, at the first session, she revealed that she had actually not binged or purged for the past three weeks, so she and I explored how she was able to make this change. Ronnie believed that she had gotten into a bad habit of binging and purging and had decided that she needed to tell her husband of ten years about her secret. After much inner turmoil, she told him and was shocked at his warm and accepting response. He told her he would do whatever she needed and that he would support her in her efforts to stop this habit.

She viewed this as the turning point in her ability to stop binging and purging. I then explored what specifically was helping her, particularly when she had the urge to binge and purge. Basically, Ronnie said, she just thought of her husband and how much he loved her. More than anything else, she did not want to let him down. She identified this specific thought and not buying binge foods as the two most helpful strategies in refraining from binging and purging.

I reinforced these solutions, complimented her for her progress, and asked, since she was doing so well, why she was coming to counseling. Ronnie said she had had periods of abstinence before, but she always had a relapse around the eleventh or twelfth week. She wanted a therapist on hand, so that if she was having a particularly difficult time at her usual relapse periods, she would have an appointment already set up. Although she really believed that this time was different because her husband now knew, she still wanted this backup plan.

We scheduled an appointment at the time Ronnie thought she might need it, but two days before then, she called to cancel, reporting that she had passed the test! She reported that she was still doing extremely well and felt confident that she could continue. She did not feel that she needed to schedule any further appointments. At both a six-month and a twelve-month follow-up, Ronnie reported continued abstinence.

This case illustrates just how rapid change can be. In fact, when therapy fosters competence, takes what the client presents at face value, and works collaboratively with the client by supporting her goals for therapy, rapid change is almost inevitable.

ASSUMPTION: *The therapist is an active participant in the process and her primary role is to identify, reinforce, and amplify change.*

Perhaps this was the most difficult mindset for me to acquire, but it was also the most significant, particularly for its impact on the eating disorder client herself. Previously, I had believed that change occurred as a result of insight and education. I was of the opinion that it was critical for the client to explore her feelings, especially her mother-rage, and to learn more appropriate ways of expressing her anger. My pathology-based mindset viewed recovery as a lifelong process in which clients would continually struggle with their addiction or eating disorder and the ravages of their dysfunctional birth families. Consequently, my treatment was unspecific, and I responded to events as they emerged from the session.

For many eating disorder clients, anorexia or bulimia has become integral to their daily lives. Clients typically report that the anorexia or bulimia is a "part" of who they are. Therapists can inadvertently deepen this client belief by focusing on the pathology or deficits related to the eating disorder, thereby spending time on that "part" of the client.

Focusing on change instead of illness is of particular importance in working with eating disorder clients for two reasons. The first has to do with their low self-esteem, a critical factor in the development and maintenance of an eating disorder. The second has to do with their tendency to employ dichotomous or all-or-none thinking through which they evaluate what they do as either good or bad. Thus, they tend both to maintain a negative view of themselves and to discount any progress that falls short of perfection. They are trapped in a negative loop of shame and self-hate fueled by the behaviors of their eating disorder, and they perceive themselves as inadequate, out of control, and defective. This is the "part" of themselves they are most familiar with.

By exploring exceptions and solution patterns, solution-focused therapists create clients' awareness of personal capabilities and resources as well as increase clients' perceptions of self-efficacy. We guide them into experiencing this *other* part of themselves. Each of the case studies I have presented here illustrates the potency of this view of the therapist's role. Unlike traditional therapists, solution-focused brief therapists envision a future for the client that is even better than the client's situation at the termination of therapy, and they see rapid change as a positive sign that more change is certain to come for the client.

However, in order for therapists to succeed with this approach, it is imperative that they reexamine their clinical assumptions regarding eating disorders, the roles of the patient and therapist, and the therapeutic process itself. This is no easy task, especially for those of us who have been trained and experientially seasoned in the psychodynamically based therapies. As a "recovering" long-term therapist, I have to continually reflect on the assumptions I have described here and challenge my old mindsets about eating disorder clients. When I find myself "stuck" with a "difficult" client, I am quick to realize I have relapsed. Usually, my relapse is related to my own mindlessness, and a careful review of my assumptions about the client and her eating disorder gently nudges me back in the right direction. Once back on track, I find therapy to be a more efficient process, since my client and I are working together as collaborators in discovering salient solutions to her complaints. We work as partners in clearly defining the focus and desired outcome of therapy and each of us then knows exactly where the finish line is. How else could we ever know if our collaboration was a success or not?

Four

The Changing
Therapeutic Relationship:
The Art of Collaboration

"You're thinking about something, my dear, and
that makes you forget to talk. I can't tell you just
now what the moral of that is, but I shall remember
it in a bit."

"Perhaps it hasn't one," Alice ventured to
remark.

"Tut, tut, child!" said the Duchess. "Everything's
got a moral, if only you can find it."

—*Lewis Carroll*
Alice's Adventures in Wonderland

All psychotherapeutic systems recognize the significant role the
therapeutic relationship plays in the overall effectiveness and outcome of treatment. The quality and dynamics of the therapeutic
relationship are especially crucial in treating eating disorder clients
for several reasons. First, for bulimics, the relationship is a determinant in the client's willingness to openly explore and discuss behavior patterns perceived as shameful and disgusting. For anorexics, the
relationship is a determinant in their willingness to consider altering their eating patterns, a frightening possibility because it would
result in weight gain. Second, the relationship affects the client's
ability to disclose accurate information about her eating and purging behaviors and weight fluctuations as well as other serious physiological symptoms.

Third, unlike other clients who readily admit that they are
experiencing a problem situation or relationship, many eating disorder clients have been coerced or strongly persuaded to seek

therapy by concerned friends or family or both. For anorexics and some bulimics, treatment is viewed as another attempt to control their relationship with food and alter their weight, thus robbing them of what they prize most. For other bulimics, treatment often appears to be a magical key to their dilemma and the only way to "purge" the malediction under which they feel they labor, consequently their level of expectation is very high. Given the tenacity of the eating disorder behaviors and bulimics' tendency toward dichotomous, perfectionist thinking and negative self-image, their hopes are often short-lived. Many clients have had therapy or have attempted changing their behavior on their own numerous times with little *perceived* success; thus, their level of confidence is enervated.

On top of all this, eating disorder clients, sometimes described as masterful people pleasers, have a penchant for saying and doing the "right" things while masking their authentic needs and desires. Thus, it is understandable that they might be perceived as displaying resistant, manipulative, defiant, and stubborn behaviors.

Treating anorexics or bulimics often generates significant feelings of frustration, inadequacy, and aggression in the therapist (Selvini-Palazzoli, 1978). According to Cohler (1977, p. 353), "Psychotherapy with anorectic patients leads to intense emotional reactions in the therapist: perhaps the most intense encountered in a therapeutic relationship."

Cohler (1977) discusses the necessity of employing behavioral manipulation as a means of dealing with the intensity of these feelings, "Considering the intensity of anger and despair evoked in the therapist by prolonged psychotherapeutic contact with anorectic patients, it is little wonder that those who find themselves in the position of having to treat such patients often have recourse to behavioral manipulation and modification. Although such behavioral approaches do not appear to yield favorable results superior to those obtained with the best intensive psychotherapy . . . , even psychodynamically oriented reports attempt to *resolve problems resulting from the therapist's frustration by recommending manipulative procedures in the treatment of anorectic patients* [italics mine] (p. 353).

Relational Adjustments

A therapist's frustration, anger, or despair is a clear indication that the client and therapist are *not* working together, rather they are engaged in some type of power struggle. The distrust and interpersonal distress experienced by both individuals impedes the establishment of a strong alliance.

In attempting to develop and maintain a cooperative posture with eating disorder clients, therapists have to become more mindful and deal with their own discomforts in making the relational adjustments necessary to practice solution-focused brief therapy. The relational adjustments involve three critical issues: power, collaboration, and faith.

Power and Collaboration

The dominant theoretical orientations of the first three waves of clinical influence—although not intrinsically motivated to achieve personal power in the therapeutic relationship—are greatly influenced by the hierarchical model of relationships, which precludes mutuality. In psychoanalytic orientations, the therapist's primary role is to serve as a self-object in order to ameliorate psychological deficits. Levenkron (1982) characterizes the eating disorder therapist as being a parent, guide, coach, and teacher. This view presupposes a hierarchical relationship between client and therapist in which the client is identified as "sick" and in need of help and the therapist is the "expert" and trained to function in the best interests of the client by assisting her to get well. Cognitive therapists focus on symptomatic behavior and work to alter the client's maladaptive cognitive structures, specifically those related to food, weight, and shape.

Granted, the nature of the therapeutic relationship sets itself apart from other human relationships and is not mutual in the sense of reciprocity. Conversations in this "for pay" relationship are centered around one person's problematic situation, and expectations are such that the individual seeking the relationship perceives the other to possess some skill or expertise that can help to alleviate the problematic situation. At one level, solution-focused therapists honor and understand the client's expectations, but at a deeper level—out of respect for the client's inherent self-regulating capacity—they abdicate the power-based role and assume the posture of student or, as Siegel (1986) calls it, "privileged listener."

Relinquishing the role of expert, with all of its dubious rights and privileges, presupposes that one can't be an expert for every human being encountered. In other words, the solution-focused therapist views each and every client as a unique human being in the context of her reality. Consequently, treatment is highly individualized. Gilligan (1990, p. 368) sums up this approach by writing, "Appreciate that your reality, your way of being, your perspective is not superior to the client's. Both therapist and client are operating in 'as if' worlds, acting 'as if' the world were this way or that way. Assuming that your 'as if' world is better or more accurate moves therapy into a competitive power play."

Given the heterogeneity of the population and the diverse and variant degrees of symptomatology (as reported in the literature), this individualization of treatment is particularly crucial in working with eating disorders clients. The solution-focused therapist treats as many different eating disorders as she has clients. As Berg and Miller (1992, p.7) state in their book on alcoholism, "Milton Erickson once said that he invented a 'new treatment in accord with the individual.' Rather than treating one alcoholism, the solution-focused therapist treats many different alcoholisms—a different type for each client that is treated."

The pejorative labels that are typically used to describe the eating disorders clients may well be a reflection of the dynamics of the hierarchical therapeutic relationship. A cooperative and mutual relationship, in which the realities of the client are acknowledged and respected, precludes resistance and recalcitrance. As discussed in Chapter Three, within a mutual, cooperative relationship, in which the therapist joins with the client, resistance is unnecessary. To quote deShazer (1985, pp. 15–16), "Over and over I found people sent to me by other therapists (complete with the label 'resistant client') to be both desperate for change and highly cooperative. . . . [The] idea that 'clients' are going to resist change is at least misguided. In fact, with this kind of idea in mind, the therapist can actually generate 'resistance' or non-cooperation, if not conflict. That is, the therapist's notions could generate a self-fulfilling prophecy with an unsuccessful outcome."

In traditional therapy, the hierarchical relationship and therapeutic process lends itself to teaching the client the clinical language of dysfunction and pathology, terms such as *codependent, enabling, separation/individuation, mother-rage, developmental crisis, developmental task, enmeshment,* and so on. Clients learn to label their deficits, assimilating themselves into the clinician's world of pathology and sickness while relinquishing their own language derived from their own experience. Such insensitivity to the client's language creates another detour on the way to cooperation and efficiency and can fuel apparent resistance.

According to Berg and Miller (1992, p. 97), "When clients have idiosyncratic ways of using words, it is helpful for the therapist to imitate and incorporate what the client says, wherever possible. This joining maneuver engenders in the client a feeling of being understood and reassured by the professional, thus reducing the client's need to defend her position."

In the case of eating disorder clients, therapy becomes unnecessarily complicated when the client identifies, for example, simply having a better relationship with her mother as a goal and the therapist assumes that the client needs to explore enmeshment and separation/individuation issues in order for that to happen. The following dialogue (from an actual session, as are all the dialogues in this book) illustrates an alternative approach in which I, as the therapist, used the client's language to probe for her view of what a normal relationship with her mother would look like.

CLIENT: My mother and I have these stupid fights over whether or not I need to go to the dentist or what I'm wearing. We have real blowups over what I eat or should I say, what I don't eat. It's just so stupid. I mean, I'm twenty-two years old for Christ's sake. She just doesn't know when to back off. I just wish we could have a more normal relationship. You know, like other mothers and daughters.

THERAPIST: So if you had a more normal relationship with your mother, like other mothers and daughters, one where she knew when to back off, how would it be different between the two of you?

CLIENT: Well, she'd be totally different. She would respect me more and realize I *do* have brains.

THERAPIST: Okay, let's pretend that your mother respects you more and realizes that you do have brains, how would you be different?

CLIENT: Oh, I'd probably not be so antagonistic towards her. I mean I would not be so weird about my privacy. I just won't tell her anything that's going on in my life. It really bugs her. I really feel guilty when I shut her out.

THERAPIST: So how could she tell that you're not being antagonistic and weird about your privacy?

CLIENT: Well, I guess my tone of voice would be softer. I wouldn't bark at her. Well, that's what she says, I bark at her. "Woof, woof" [laughs].

THERAPIST: So your voice would be softer. What else is different when you're not barking?

I then continued to work with this client in defining her view of the difference she wants to see in her relationship with her mother, using the client's idiosyncratic descriptors in the process. Replacing client language descriptors with clinical language not only promotes unnecessary detours but also can fuel subtle power struggles that keep clients distrustful and suspicious of therapists' motives. Developing a cooperative client-therapist relationship is the cornerstone of the solution-focused model. Erickson (1965, p. 59) himself says, "Merely to make a correct diagnosis of the illness and to know the correct method of treatment is not enough. Fully as important is that the patient be receptive of the therapy and cooperative in regard to it. Without the patient's full cooperativeness, therapeutic results are delayed, distorted, limited or even prevented."

Compliance in treatment is significantly increased when the therapist cooperates with the client and permits her to establish and work toward goals that are salient to her (Hester & Miller, 1989; Miller, 1985). This can be particularly difficult when the client's goals may, at some stage of her treatment, appear to be medically dangerous to her well-being or are in opposition to the therapist's values related to weight and eating. However, the solution-focused therapist, in having established a mutual, collaborative relationship and utilizing the *client's* solution patterns, can neutralize the power struggle that only serves to exacerbate the problematic situation. This allows treatment to proceed more efficiently. Thus, relinquishing the power base and deferring to the client is a critical first step in establishing a cooperative, mutual relationship.

Faith

Another relational adjustment involves the therapist's belief about the self-healing and self-regulating capacity of the human organism. One of the critical aspects of living-systems theory is the concept of a cybernetic process in which there is a dynamic process of self-regulatory feedback loops. According to Seeman (1989, p. 350), a fundamental proposition related to adaptive processes is that living systems have self-regulating properties. "This concept of lawfulness and self-regulation through cybernetic processes is a keystone of human-system theory. Following from this view, the concept of positive health rests on the premise that efficacy in self-regulation provides superior resources of growth, maintenance, and survival to the human organism. Similarly, the concept of failure in self-regulation represents a basic construct for understanding disease. In this sense, for instance, iatrogenic disease can be understood as an unsuccessful intrusion by a professional into the self-regulative mechanisms."

Again using the analogy of the homeopathic approach to medicine, which stresses the value of working *with* the body and its own natural healing powers, this relational adjustment requires a faith in the client's natural self-healing capacities. Friedman and Fanger (1991, p. 15) state, "We view the therapist as a guide who takes his cues from the client and relies on the client's natural momentum towards movement and change. The therapist needs to have faith in the healing power contained within the client's natural healing ecology."

Instead of believing that the therapist needs to assume many different roles such as teacher, coach, parent, or advisor, as Levenkron (1982) suggests, becoming a collaborator, student, and privileged listener can diminish the negative feelings often experienced by both therapist and client. This relational adjustment requires faith and humility on the part of the therapist and is particularly difficult to make in the treatment of eating disorder clients, as they are incredibly creative in their challenges to the therapist's ideas about normal eating patterns.

A case study illustrates how the therapist constructs a cooperative relationship with the client.

Case Study

"Rio," a forty-two-year-old married woman with two children sought counseling for her anorexia. She had a history of problems with eating and with weight that ranged from obese to anorexic levels. She had sought treatment on several occasions but dropped out when she felt she was not really getting anywhere.

When Rio came to EDRC, she was seeking treatment because she herself was concerned about her low weight. Six months prior, she had felt more comfortable about her eating, which had included an "addiction" to bagels and popcorn. Recently, she found herself unable to even eat these favorite foods and was purging after her evening meal of beer and lettuce. She was beginning to experience pain in her bones from any extended sitting or sleeping and was embarrassed about how she was beginning to look. She was going to a sales meeting and knew she needed to gain weight so she would not be the subject of concern from her employer and peers. The goal she identified was that she wanted to start eating as she used to and to stop purging altogether. She was, of course, terrified of gaining weight and felt that if she stopped purging she would get "fat" again.

Rio revealed that most recently she had begun eating breakfast (osterized cottage cheese) and lunch (fat-free yogurt or skim milk), which was highly unusual for her, but she desperately wanted to eat more. During the course of the interview, she identified other significant changes she had been making; however, she did not think of them as important until I amplified and highlighted their significance. In addition to "drinking" her breakfast and lunch, she had decided to allow herself to use 1 percent cottage cheese (a major change, since she reported that she was obsessive about fat content) and had decided to skip exercise every other day. I complimented Rio for her hard work and reinforced the significance of the changes she had made.

During the first session, Rio and I agreed that maintaining her breakfast and lunch regimen would be the goal of treatment at this time. She recognized that stopping her purging would be much too difficult. She wanted to make sure she could keep some nutrients down without purging but quickly added that she knew she could not do this in the evening. I agreed with her and supported her goal for treatment. As this client continued to work, and work she did, at achieving her goal, and as she gained confidence in her ability to eat during the day, she eventually increased her food intake by adding fruit to her daily regimen.

This case emphasizes the third relational adjustment required of therapists, the ability to transcend their personal value and belief systems and thus suspend their judgments. This can be particularly difficult when it comes to therapists' values and beliefs surrounding food, eating patterns, and weight. We therapists all have our own relationships with food as well as our own viewpoints of what constitutes a healthy diet and exercise regimen, and we tend to use this standard as a measure in our treatment of eating disorder clients. However, we need to be particularly sensitive to these biases and allow our clients to determine the quality of their own nutritional lives.

At the numerous workshops on eating disorders that I have conducted over the years, many therapists have reported to me that they have a stronger sense of urgency in working with an anorexic client and trying to "get her to eat" than they do when treating an obese client and trying to "get her to lose weight," in spite of the fact that both clients can suffer from serious medical complications as a result of their respective weight levels. As long as an individual is being medically monitored and her weight is not at a medically critical point, it is intrusive and somewhat arrogant for us to actively interfere with that individual's expressed goals or solutions. If we face our own biases related to weight, eating, and body shape, we are better able to foster a collaborative relationship with clients, respecting the choices they make in determining the quality of their own lives.

Often, as the client and I deconstruct the problem, the client's goals may not even address the eating behaviors initially identified as the complaint; thus, treatment may not even focus on the anorexic or bulimic behaviors. In my experience, this happens more times than not. However, the fundamental assumption I have described about the ripple effects of change makes it possible for me to accept the client's goals even when they do not address the initial complaint. This case study shows how one goal can lead to another.

Case Study

"Hally," a forty-eight-year-old mother of three, two girls aged ten and eight and an adolescent boy age fourteen, sought treatment because she wanted to stop binging and purging. Hally was a graphic artist and took great pride in her creative talents. As an adolescent, she had had a history of bulimia, but had done well during her twenties and thirties (which according to her meant she was binging and purging only a few times a month). Now, however, these episodes happened on a daily basis.

In an exploration of exceptions, she and I identified that she binged and purged in the evenings but she did not binge and purge on the evenings when she and her son, "Jed," "got along," which was happening less and less. She described getting along as Jed's doing the dishes without being told and their being able to carry on a decent conversation about the day's events. On those days that she binged and purged, she and Jed had had a conflict, usually about his not doing the dishes. She said she felt awful when they fought, and while doing "his dishes," would binge and then go upstairs and throw up.

I asked her if she would be willing to do something different the next time things started to get heated between her and her son. When she asked what that different behavior would be, I told her I felt confident that she could come up with something "creative" (this was the adjective she used to describe herself repeatedly throughout our session). At our next session, three weeks later, Hally reported that her binging and purging episodes had dramatically decreased. After our previous session, she had decided she simply was not going to fight with her son. So when he refused to do the dishes the very next evening, instead of yelling, getting into an heated argument with him, and then doing "his dishes," she decided to say nothing, take a walk instead, and just "let those dishes rot if need be." When she returned, to her amazement the dishes were done. When she asked her husband who had done the dishes, he replied that, after somewhat of an argument, he and Jed had ended up doing them together and that Jed had asked if he could do a different household chore. He said that he hated to do dishes and would do just about anything else, so they worked out a trade-off with his younger sister, whose job it was to set the table and sweep the floor.

According to Hally, Jed still needed to be reminded about his responsibilities, but things were much better. There was much less fighting, and she did much less binging and purging. She felt more in control of her eating and did not feel a need to continue with treatment. Therefore, therapy ended with this second session.

To summarize, there are three basic strategies that promote a cooperative, trusting therapeutic relationship within the short time span of brief therapy.

1. The therapist needs to develop a keen curiosity regarding each and every client. Much like a visitor to a foreign country who initially spends time familiarizing himself or herself with the customs and the language, the therapist must develop a willingness to be curious about the client's reality.

2. The therapist needs to be sensitive to the client's use of language and to incorporate the client's idiosyncratic expressions into the therapeutic conversation, showing a particular sensitivity to her descriptors of her eating problem. Thus, if the client refers to her problematic eating behaviors as "an addiction," "a bad habit," or "an obsession," the therapist needs to accept this view and to refer to the eating behaviors in the same terms.

3. The therapist must be sensitive to goals that are salient to the client and refrain from passing judgment, especially in regard to food choices or eating patterns. Although a therapist cannot promote behaviors that are medically dangerous, negotiations in cooperative relationships can often minimize clients' self-destructive choices.

To achieve such results, therapists learning to use brief therapy must be hypervigilant regarding issues of power, clients' self-healing capacity and inner resourcefulness, and the therapists' own values regarding eating, weight, and body shape. Cooperation between client and therapist is also crucial if therapy is to be successful. This is particularly true in the solution-focused model, since the solution-focused therapist *assumes* the client is cooperating and actively looks for cooperative behaviors (deShazer, 1985), attempting "to establish conditions under which cooperating will be promoted in the very first session" (p. 74). Cooperation can be fostered when the therapist has an understanding of the varieties of relationships that are possible with eating disorder clients and also a model that identifies the various stages clients pass through as their behaviors and attitudes change.

Perhaps one of the most useful aspects of the solution-focused model in its application to eating disorders is its conceptualization of the different client-therapist relationships that are possible. When applied in clinical practice, these ways of viewing the relationship can greatly reduce the frustration and anger eating disorder therapists frequently experience. The types of relationships are (Berg & Miller, 1992; deShazer, 1988):

- Customer
- Complainant
- Visitor

These three types describe interactions between client and therapist (Berg & Miller, 1992). They do *not* describe solely the client. Moreover, the type of relationship that applies is determined by *both* therapist and the client. However, the major responsibility for type of relationship that emerges rests with the therapist (Berg & Miller, 1992). Also, these relationship types are not fixed but fluid and spontaneous, because the client is changing.

The solution-focused model rejects not only the notion of resistance but also the concept of the client's inherent readiness for change. In eschewing inherent client motivation, deShazer (1985) emphasizes the interactional concept of compatibility between the therapist and the client as much more clinically useful. However, I have found it extremely effective to use a model of change concomitantly with a knowledge of relationship types. This model assists the therapist in developing a better sense of not only the relationship but also the client's level of motivation.

Motivation is not defined here as a client trait or personality characteristic. According to Miller (1989), a psychologist in the addictions field, problems of motivation are problems of compliance. Thus, motivation is not something one *has* but rather what one *does*. Prochaska and DiClemente (1982) have attempted to understand why and how people change their behavior, either alone or with the help of a professional. Based on their research with smokers, they delineate five stages of change that people go through in altering troubled or problematic behavior, and their model is the one I have found useful. (This change model applies to people whether or not they are in therapy.) The five stages are

- Precontemplation
- Contemplation
- Determination
- Action
- Maintenance/Relapse

While the relationship type can change throughout the course of even one session, these stages of change are a predictable and stable subprocess within the therapeutic process (see Figure 4.1).

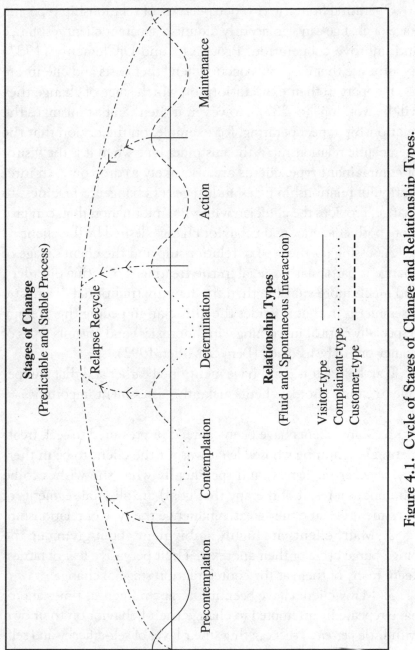

Figure 4.1. Cycle of Stages of Change and Relationship Types.

Operating from the two perspectives of relationship type and stage of change can significantly diminish apparent client resistance and improve cooperation. Prochaska and DiClemente (1982) hypothesize that drop-outs occur when "therapists and clients are too far apart in their expectations on which stage of change they will be working" (p. 287). However, if the therapist mistakes the relationship type, operating, for example, on the notion that the therapeutic relationship is the customer type when it is the visitor or complainant type, clients are also likely to drop out. An integration of relationship types and stages of change, or readiness to change, provides the clinician with vital information than can promote both efficiency and behavior change desired by the client.

Assessing for the type of relationship and the client's stage of change is particularly crucial in the treatment of eating disorders, and much more valuable than the lengthy traditional diagnostic assessment, in that it guides the clinician in pacing the therapy (especially critical in working with anorexics) and suggests types of homework to be assigned (Berg & Miller, 1992).

Four key factors that I have mentioned earlier and that are specific to eating disorder clients make this assessment important.

1. Many clients have been coerced or pressured to seek treatment. Determining whose idea it was for the client to be in therapy, *whether she agrees*, and specifically what she wishes to be different as a result of therapy (her goal) are all vital segments of assessment because they greatly influence the type of relationship.

2. Many clients are highly ambivalent about giving up the binge-purge cycle or their anorexia. Their pervasive fear of fatness keeps many of them at the contemplation stage of change.

3. Many clients have been in therapy numerous times and/or have repeatedly attempted to change their behavior on their own with little *perceived* success; thus, their level of self-efficacy and self-confidence is greatly impaired and their increasing fear of failure can restrain them from moving out of the contemplation stage.

4. Many clients tend to discount or ignore those times they have been able to manage their problem eating behaviors. Identifying the times they have operated within the action stage of change increases their perceptions of self-efficacy and this improved self-perception (according to Prochaska and DiClemente's research, 1982) has a significant effect on their continued success in managing the behaviors.

By being responsive to the rhythms of the relationship and the client's readiness, and thus establishing *a client-determined focus for therapy*, the therapist not only makes the best use of therapy time but also, and most importantly, fosters deeper client trust and cooperativeness within the relationship. This trust and cooperation also serves as a catalyst for change.

The following section explores more fully the stages of change and the relationship type that corresponds to each stage.

Precontemplation Stage and Visitor Relationship

Individuals in the precontemplation stage are not even thinking about altering their behavior. In fact, they do not believe their eating or restricting is a problem and discount what significant others say about the behaviors. Precontemplation individuals are often labeled as resistant or in denial. Prochaska and DiClemente (1982) delineate four types of precontemplators.

1. Reluctant precontemplators, as a result of either ignorance or inertia, simply do not consider change. Generally, they are not fully conscious of the implications of the problematic behavior.

2. Rebellious precontemplators are generally hostile to and resistant to change. Generally strongly entrenched in the problematic behavior, they defy being told what to do.

3. Resigned precontemplators are passively lethargic, with a sense of hopelessness and general feelings of being overwhelmed by the problem. They typically feel out of control.

4. Rationalizing precontemplators have all the answers and know exactly why the problem is not a problem or why it is a problem for others but not for them (DiClemente, 1991).

Eating disorder clients fall mainly into the categories of rebellious and resigned precontemplators. When confronted about their behaviors, anorexic or bulimic precontemplators are sometimes initially surprised but more often defensive, and this defensiveness intensifies if the individual is coerced into seeking treatment. Anorexic precontemplators tend to be mired in the fear of losing control, whereas bulimic precontemplators tend to be fearful of being exposed.

During the precontemplation stage of change, the therapist needs to be particularly sensitive to the client's fears and must first seek to join with the client by acknowledging her feelings. The therapist needs to provide basic information to the client regarding both the short-term and long-term physiological consequences of anorexia and bulimia and must seek to discover if the client wishes to use therapy in any other way. Giving prescriptive advice, probing, or any other type of therapeutic maneuvering is counterproductive and will more than likely heighten the client's distrust of the therapist.

Typically, precontemplators participate in visitor-type relationships; however, this can change depending upon whether the client and therapist can negotiate another client-identified goal.

A precontemplator in the visitor relationship

- Is uncommitted and is seeking therapy under some duress (usually specifically as a result of pressure from concerned family members or friends)
- Is unable to develop, jointly with the therapist, a complaint or goal on which to work
- Generally believes that she has no problem or the problem belongs to someone else
- Sees no reason for therapy

The therapist working with a precontemplator in the visitor relationship has six tasks. In the first three tasks, the therapist

- Actively and respectfully listens to the client's plight and sympathizes with her
- Works with those significant others who choose to participate
- Uses compliments as appropriate and leaves the door open, inviting the client back if, in the future, the client feels the therapist can be helpful to her

The remaining three tasks require fuller explanations.

- Do nothing, provide basic education, work with concerned family members who choose to participate.

Many eating disorder clients seek treatment under pressure from significant others, and in this situation, the therapist initially needs to ask the client if she *agrees* with the significant other. The precontemplator will generally say no. The therapist should either agree with the client's viewpoint or take no particular stance on whether or not she has an eating disorder. Moreover, if this client and the therapist are also unable to identify any non-eating-related complaint or problem that is meaningful to the client, the therapist should not suggest any interventions since the client does not, in the client's view, have a problem (Berg & Miller, 1992). The therapist can provide basic information to this client regarding the physiological effects of starvation and binging and purging, in order to raise her awareness level. However, again, anything more than this can heighten client distrust.

In providing basic information, the therapist must adopt a benign, not a prescriptive manner (Miller & Rollnick, 1991), and the therapist must not manipulate, cajole or coerce the client into treatment compliance. At EDRC, all clients receive a simple handout that outlines the negative effects of dieting and starvation on metabolism, discusses other individual differences (gender, body surface area, and exercise) that affect metabolic rates, and describes some basic guidelines for weight loss and maintenance.

Quite often when the therapist accepts the precontemplator's view that there is no problem or not that much of a problem, the client returns at a later date. The case study of Rae (Chapter Two) is an excellent example of this principle. The therapist also can focus her attention on those individuals in the client system who are wanting help. In other words, instead of trying to "sell" the client who is not interested in "buying," the therapist can work with those members of the client's family system who *have* demonstrated a desire to participate in the process.

- Determine if the client is a customer for another complaint; one that is salient to her.

Since eating disorder clients in the precontemplation stage frequently do not identify their eating or restricting behaviors as problems and, in fact, take great pride in their level of self-discipline, the solution-focused therapist works *with* the client to determine if there is another complaint or goal on which the client wishes to work and for which she can become a customer (Berg & Miller, 1992).

Case Study

"Jahna," a twenty-three-year-old anorexic woman, sought counseling under great pressure from her husband. She didn't see any problem with her weight and thought her eating and exercise regimen was just fine. She reported that she did not want to be in counseling, since she was quite happy with her weight and would really be elated when she lost ten more pounds. As the interview progressed, she indicated that she and her husband, married only a few years, were having terrible fights about her eating and exercise and that she would get very angry with him because he treated her like a child, "always watching what I eat, telling me what I should eat, and yelling at me when I don't eat enough."

Finally, her complaint regarding her husband's treatment of her emerged as a complaint that she wanted to work on. Thus, our relationship shifted into a customer one, in which we first explored exceptions, discussing those times her husband treated her like an adult, which in some instances occurred when she ate more. As the interview progressed, we also identified what she would have to do differently so that her spouse would be less likely to treat her like a child. That is, rather than confronting or even discussing this client's eating behaviors, a tactic that would have generated only feelings of resistance, the client and I, together, identified a complaint that was salient to her and that moved our visitor-type relationship to a customer-type relationship. Consequently, the client was more cooperative and continued in therapy. By the fifth session, she moved into the contemplation stage of change regarding her eating disorder and was willing to take a look at her eating behaviors, which then became the central focus of treatment.

• Join with the client in her desire to discontinue counseling.

A key task for the therapist in working with visitors-precontemplators who have been coerced into treatment is to empathize with their distress about being in counseling and ask them what it would take or what would have to happen so that they would not have to continue in counseling (Miller, 1992b). Taking this approach promotes cooperation, since the therapist and the client agree on the client's desire to terminate.

According to DiClemente (1991), there are two major possible pitfalls in dealing with individuals in the stage of precontemplation. One is to assume that the problem behavior means the same thing to the client as it does to the therapist. In the case of eating disorder clients, therapists must not lose sight of the pervasive and painfully powerful fear of fatness that fuels the maladaptive eating behaviors. It is very easy to become entangled in a power struggle with the client over food intake or an exercise regimen. The therapist must maintain a deep empathy and sensitivity to the client's reality, including her terror of weight gain. Moreover, the therapist's recognition and acceptance of the client's reality diminishes power struggles and negative feelings.

Anorexics have been identified as extremely resistant and controlling clients. Yet in our work at the EDRC, my colleagues and I have found that by assessing for client motivational stage and relationship type and by identifying a goal important to the client, anorexics pose no greater challenge than any other client. Here is a typical conversation with an anorexic during the first session of solution-focused therapy.

THERAPIST: So you are only here because Dr. "Jones" [the client's pediatrician] and your folks think you need to gain weight? Is that right?

CLIENT [*nodding her head*]: Uh huh.

THERAPIST: What do you think?

CLIENT: I don't think I have a problem with eating. I do just fine. I'm just like anybody else.

THERAPIST: Well, can you help me out here? I'm kinda confused. Weren't you hospitalized last spring because of your low weight level?

CLIENT: Yeah. I hated that place. It was awful.

THERAPIST: I can imagine how tough that must have been. So why do you suppose you were put in there?

CLIENT [*in a lowered voice*]: 'Cause I wasn't eating. [*More animatedly.*] But things got better and I don't know why I have to come here or go to Dr. Jones's for weigh-ins. Things are much better now.

THERAPIST: Tell me how you think things are much better.

CLIENT: Well, I got as high as ninety-five pounds.

THERAPIST: What do you weigh now?

CLIENT: I'm at what Dr. Jones calls a borderline weight of ninety-one pounds. She says if I lose just a quarter-pound I have to go back to the hospital.

THERAPIST: That wouldn't be too much fun. So how did you get as high as ninety-five pounds?

CLIENT: I'm not gaining any more weight. I'm just fine.

THERAPIST: I was just curious. Well, it sounds like you have a real dilemma.

CLIENT: Yeah, I do. [*Pauses. Tearfully.*] I don't ever want to go back to that hospital again. I'm sick of all of these doctors. I just want to be left alone.

THERAPIST: Well, what do you suppose would have to happen so you wouldn't have to go to the hospital or see another doctor again?

CLIENT [*pauses*]: I'd have to be healthy.

THERAPIST: Yeah. So what will that take.

CLIENT: I would have to stay at ninety-two pounds. But it's really hard. I'm really afraid of getting fat.

At this point, the therapist and client began to form a customer-type relationship in which they identified a goal that was salient to the client: keeping her out of the hospital. The therapist learned from the client what it would take in order for her to reach this goal, rather than telling the client what she had to do. This goal was reached by probing for the exception related to the client's weight increase to ninety-five pounds. There is no power struggle since it is the client who has identified what she has to do and who is directed by the therapist to focus on the time she was able to gain weight. This exception could then be used to develop a solution to the client's current dilemma.

Since joining with a client in her goal produces more cooperation, therapy has a much greater chance of maintaining itself, with the client's being more open to the process and eventually moving into the contemplation stage of change.

The second potential pitfall in working with clients in the pre-contemplation stage is described this way by DiClemente (1991): "There is a myth among interviewers that in dealing with serious health-related addictive, or other problems, more is always better. More education, more intense treatment, more confrontation will necessarily produce more change. Nowhere is this less true than with the precontemplators" (p. 194). Many eating disorder clients are precontemplators in visitor-type relationships with their therapists. When the therapists focus on the pathology of these clients and on unraveling the whys of their illnesses, they are assuming that the clients are customers for this course of treatment, when in fact the client is not a customer for any treatment. It is as a result of this major discrepancy between the views of client and therapist that eating disorder clients have been maligned as resistant, stubborn, defiant, noncompliant, manipulative, and deceptive, to mention just a few of the descriptors that permeate not only the literature but also the hearts of most clinicians.

Those therapists who continue to provide therapy to precon-templators in a visitor-type relationship will only perpetuate feelings of anger, failure, and inadequacy within themselves and their clients.

Contemplation Stage and Complainant-Type Relationship

According to DiClemente (1991), contemplation is a paradoxical stage of change, since the client is open to the possibility of change but is beset by ambivalence. The characteristic style of the contemplator is, "yes, but . . ." This is the stage in which clients are "waiting for one final piece of information that will compel them to change. The hope is that the information will make the decision for them" (p. 195). Generally, the contemplator vacillates between reasons for changing and reasons for staying the same.

This stage is not quite that obvious with some eating disorder clients because they frequently say that they unequivocally want to stop binging, purging, or restricting; however, they are truly stuck where they are since they believe the solution lies outside of themselves. What compounds the situation is that their ambivalence frequently centers around their deep and pervasive feelings of inadequacy in relation to their eating and purging patterns. The dilemma for the therapist is that even though these clients blame themselves for their eating problem they generally believe its "cure" will come as a result of some magical insight or that therapy itself will "fix" them.

Prochaska and DiClemente (1982) find that individuals can stall within a stage and that "obsessives tend to become bogged down in a prolonged contemplation of a problem" (p. 283). They postulate that these individuals prefer to believe that if they think enough about an issue, sooner or later the information will lead them to the perfect solution. In my observation, another factor that perpetuates their stay in the contemplative stage is their high expectation for treatment and for themselves. They expect nothing more than total abstinence from the problem behavior to result and become greatly self-disparaging and discouraged when a relapse occurs. The relapse then results in increased ambivalence and reaffirmation of their defectiveness.

Two key techniques of the solution-focused model are critical in facilitating a shift from the contemplation stage to the determination stage of change. The first technique is asking the miracle question, to help the client identify how her life would be different if her eating disorder were miraculously gone. With this probe, the therapist can create not only an expectancy of change in the client but also, and more importantly, a sense of hopefulness about the future. The second technique is the search for exceptions. By focusing on those times she has been able to manage her problematic eating behaviors more successfully, the client in the contemplative stage of change is more likely not only to gain an awareness of her need to *do* something to create change but also to experience a greater sense of personal efficacy. As the therapeutic conversation focuses on do-able solutions, the client also begins to acquire a more realistic set of personal and therapeutic outcome expectations. (Traditional therapy, however, tends to perpetuate the eating disorder client's fantasy that the magic of change lies in the talking rather than in the doing.)

Once again, if the therapist operates as though the client in the contemplation stage is in the action stage of change, thus positing a customer-type relationship, resistance is likely to occur and the client's ambivalence to be heightened.

Contemplators tend to participate in complainant-type relationships. In these relationships, the client

- Working jointly with the therapist, has been able to identify a goal or complaint that she can usually describe in great detail
- Does *not* see herself as a part of the solution and may believe someone else has to change in order for her problem to be solved
- Is 'stuck'; focuses excessively on the problem and thinks talking about the problem will solve it
- Frequently indicates she knows what she needs to do or what should be different but is unwilling to take any specific action or vacillates about what to do first

The therapist in the complainant relationship has these tasks: he or she

- Agrees to explore the complaint further with the client in order to negotiate a solvable problem for which the client would enter a customer relationship
- Employs specific skills to help client see a *new* view of the problem
- Empowers client to take action

The therapist does not assign any "doing" tasks to the client at this stage, but may assign an observing or reflecting task (Miller, 1992b). Many parents of anorexics or bulimics engage in complainant relationships in which the youngster's eating, exercise, and social behaviors form the target of the therapeutic conversation, with much discussion of the problem but no attempt by the youngster to see herself as part of a solution.

In working within a complainant-type relationship, the therapist should minimize discussions related to the problem and gently guide the client to an exploration of solutions. The therapeutic task is to empower clients by raising their awareness of what is possible and achievable within the contexts of their current situations, as the next example shows.

Case Study

"Randi," a twenty-year-old bulimic, sought counseling because she was "sick and tired" of her bulimia. She binged and purged three to five times a day and was feeling extremely out of control. As she talked about her bulimia, she focused on the details of her history of the disorder and the problems she had with her older sister, who continually berated her for this "disgusting and weird hang-up."

During the course of the first interview, Randi continued to focus on her lack of willpower and her desire to move out of her house so she could get away from her sister. She focused on how she hated her sister, and said her wish was that her sister would just leave her alone and stop "acting like my mother." When asked which was more pressing, her relationship with her sister or her binging and purging, the client emphatically stated she wanted to work on her bulimia and stop binging and purging. She was getting tired of it and how it interfered in her life. During the course of the interview, she was unable to identify any exceptions. She just wanted to stop binging and purging. She said to me, "That's why I came here. So you could help me do that."

Randi, operating in the contemplation stage of change regarding her bulimia, had a complaint and a goal that she wished to work on; however, she did not see herself as a part of the solution to her problem. To help her develop a new view of the problem, thus freeing her from the trap of her linear thinking, I asked Randi to pay attention to the times she was not binging and purging, note what was different about those times, and report her observations at the following session.

When Randi returned for her second session, she was able to report two times when she was able to control her binging and purging and identify what was different about those times. What struck Randi was that her sister was in the house on the two occasions she identified as exceptions. She commented, "I always thought that my sister was the cause of my bulimia, but you know, I am really surprised that she's around when I don't binge and purge. Maybe she doesn't have anything to do with it after all." I amplified and highlighted those exceptional times. And Randi's awareness of the exceptions helped her develop a new view of an aspect of her complaint and began moving her toward the next stage of change.

Determination Stage and Customer Relationship

The client's willingness to take appropriate steps to alter the problem behavior or to initiate positive behaviors characterizes this stage of change. Miller & Rollnick (1991) emphasize that this stage is "something like a window of opportunity, which opens for a period of time" (p. 17). If the client takes action at this point, she will continue the change process. If not, she will regress to contemplation. The task of the therapist when the client is in the determination stage of change is "not one of motivating so much as matching—helping him or her find a change strategy that is acceptable, accessible, appropriate and effective" (p. 17).

Searching for exceptions is particularly useful in this stage, since it focuses the client on identifying both previous solution patterns and current periods of time when the problematic behaviors are not occurring. Because these exceptions are already a part of the client's repertoire of behaviors, they can be employed as strategies during the determination stage. This is a critical stage of change, since the therapist can facilitate either progression or regression, based on the type of questions asked and strategies employed.

Eating disorder clients in this stage are willing to take action and work hard to bring about change. They begin to have an understanding of the concept of choice as it relates to their problematic eating behaviors, and they are becoming more aware of the real consequences of their choices. It is the therapist's task to negotiate with these clients and assist them in developing salient, realistic, and achievable goals.

Typically, individuals in the determination stage of change participate in customer-type relationships. The concept of the customership was first proposed by the Brief Therapy Center group in Palo Alto, California (Fisch, Weakland, & Segal, 1982; Weakland, Fisch, Watzlawick, & Bodin, 1974; Watzlawick, Weakland, & Fisch, 1974) and then adapted by deShazer (Berg & Miller, 1992; deShazer, 1988).

In a customer relationship, the client

- Has initiated treatment of her own accord
- Has established the complaint or goal jointly and collaboratively with the therapist and is able to give a relatively clear description of the complaint, which may be about herself or someone else
- Sees herself as a part of the solution
- Is willing to take steps to build a solution
- Becomes a doer

The therapist

- Agrees with the client's goal
- Believes she can assist the client in finding a solution
- Uses therapeutic skills to direct the client toward solutions

The therapist also assigns a "doing" task to the client in this stage, because the customer relationship is one in which the client is motivated and open to treatment (Miller, 1992b). As clients become doers, they also become willing to take responsibility for their complaints. Rio, the forty-two-year-old anorexic in one of the cases described earlier, is a good example of a client in a customer relationship in that she identified herself as a part of the solution and was motivated and willing to do something to change her situation.

Contrary to the widely held view that eating disorder clients tend to be resistant and uncooperative or difficult to treat, in my clinical experience I have found these clients to be like any others. This is largely due to my assessing each client's stage of change and then resonating with the type of relationship we form. I become a collaborator who is interested in focusing on the client's goals and utilizing her solutions or exceptions patterns, as happened in the next example.

Case Study

"Mikki" was a twenty-nine-year-old nurse who had been anorexic since adolescence. She had had numerous hospitalizations as a youngster and extensive outpatient therapy. She reported that although her eating was not nearly as restrictive as it once had been, she still worried about getting fat and struggled in her relationship with food. In spite of these difficulties, she had graduated from high school, attended nursing school, and eventually received her master's degree, with no financial or emotional support from her family.

At this point in her life, she had an excellent job which she loved and was beginning to form a circle of friends she felt good about.

She sought counseling because her eating was becoming more and more restrictive and her purging activities were increasing, and she did not want to "lose everything" she "worked so hard to get." She was well aware that if she continued in her current pattern of eating, her job performance would be impaired, since she was already beginning to have difficulty concentrating, and frequently felt dizzy, lightheaded, and faint. She had a very responsible position in acute patient care services, and she felt she was not doing her patients any good at this time.

Whenever her parents came to visit her, she would experience a great deal of anxiety and stress regarding her contact with them, and as a result, her eating patterns would generally become more restrictive than usual. She reported that her father had sexually abused her but that when she disclosed this to her mother a few years ago, her mother simply did not believe her and did not talk to her for a few months until she retracted her accusation—which she did "just to keep peace." Since Thanksgiving was coming up in a few months, and her parents would be visiting her, she felt she needed some support to get through the months before their visit. Once they left, she knew things would return to normal for her. She repeated that she just needed some help over the next few months.

It was clear that her job was extremely important to her. Thus, I asked her what she would have to do differently so her work performance could return to its usual level.

She thought a long time before she said, "Well, I know I can't completely stop throwing up for now. I know that." To her great surprise, I agreed with her and told her that trying to just stop probably was not a good idea. So I asked her again what would have to be different so she could feel better about her work performance.

"Well, first of all," she said, "I have to eat more. Right now, I'm only eating crackers and beer and then throwing up. I need to eat more. I know that's what I need to do. And I can do it; I've done it before." That statement in combination with similar remarks revealed that Mikki saw herself as a part of the solution to her problem and was willing to take some action to create change. In a search for exceptions, we discovered that she always ate more "normally" when she was out with her friends, and was less likely to purge afterward. However, in our conversation, she revealed that lately she had noticed she had been isolating more and more and was refusing to go out with friends. During the course of our conversation, she agreed that she would initiate two social contacts and go out for dinner with two of her closest friends and eat normally (for her, this meant a salad with no fat dressing and one dinner roll) at these two meals. She agreed to pay attention to what was different when she was with her friends, since she was confident that she was less likely to purge, and then report her observations back to me.

In this case, Mikki actively sought counseling of her own accord and was in the determination stage of change. She was able to describe what needed to be different and, in response to other questions, indicated that she was motivated to complete the task. I did not explore the sex abuse issue since that was *not* what the client wanted to address. (This is a good example of applying rule 1 of solution-focused therapy: "If it ain't broke, don't fix it." Mikki entered a customer relationship because of her desire to keep her job, a desire which, according to her, meant she had to eat more. Thus, I used this global goal in helping her identify specific strategies, based on her exceptions, that she could apply in order to preserve her job.

Action Stage

As a midwife to the process of change, the therapist must continually assess the relationship and the client's readiness for change so that an appropriate and meaningful goal can be set. Once this goal is jointly established by the therapist and the client, and the client is willing to take action to bring about change, she has entered the action stage of change.

This piece of the therapeutic process is the one that many therapists find the most gratifying. It is an extension of the determination stage. The client is reporting changes and is achieving her goals. The task of the therapist is to simply amplify, reinforce, and highlight those actions and interactions that are central to the behavior change, since this technique redefines those actions and interactions. To promote self-efficacy, the solution-focused brief therapist actively maintains the focus of treatment by asking appropriate questions about the changes the client is making relative to the specified goal and what she needs to keep doing in order to maintain those changes.

Traditional treatment is nonspecific: thus progress is generally not discussed. The solution-focused brief therapist is highly directive. By emphasizing those situations, behaviors, or circumstances that are better or different, the therapist keeps the client focused on her goal and her progress as evidenced by the treatment gains she has made.

THERAPIST: So what's better since I've seen you?

CLIENT: Well, everything's pretty good. I mean, I still haven't binged or purged. It's been six weeks now.

THERAPIST: That's terrific. Now, tell me how you have been able to maintain this very significant change.

CLIENT: Well, I just don't do it. It's like not even an option any more. I mean there have been times I've had the urge, but I just don't do it.

THERAPIST: So, what do you do differently now when you have the urge?

CLIENT: I just get busy and do something else.

THERAPIST: Good. So think of the most recent time you have had an urge and run me through in detail what you did differently.

CLIENT: Let's see. I guess it was about a week ago. Yeah, . . . last Saturday. Dick was gone, and that's always when I used to binge and purge. When he wouldn't be home.

THERAPIST: Yeah.

CLIENT: So, let's see. I really wanted to binge badly at first. But I didn't have any of my usual binge foods in the house. I just make myself not buy that crap anymore. That really helps.

THERAPIST: Well, that surely helps. But you could have gone out and bought some like you used to do. So how come you didn't?

CLIENT: I just told myself I wasn't going to break this chain of success that I've had. And that if I did, I would have to tell Dick, and he would be really disappointed in me.

THERAPIST: Wait, let me get this straight. So you talked to yourself? Is that right?

CLIENT: Yeah, that's exactly what I did. I told myself that I wasn't going to break the chain, and I thought about how badly I'd feel. Not only physically but about myself, period. My throat would usually kill me after a purge, and I'd end up feeling like shit about myself. So, I went outside and took ten deep breaths and did what worked before. I refocused on how much better I feel when I take care of myself. And I told myself I was worth it! [*Laughs.*]

THERAPIST: That's really great. You should be very proud of yourself. On a scale of 0 to 10, how confident are you that you can keep doing what you have been doing these past six weeks?

CLIENT: Oh, that's easy! An 8. I am really confident.

THERAPIST: So tell me again what it is you have to do to keep your chain of success going?

In this session, the therapist enlarged upon the changes the client had made in achieving her goal and specifically repeated the client's language ("chain of success") in solidifying client gains.

Here are three specific techniques for expanding client changes.

1. Summarize and slowly repeat the changes to the client so she can hear them ("Wait a minute. Let me get this straight. Instead of binging yesterday, you first said to yourself, 'I am not going to do this anymore!' Then you thought about the consequences—like how sore your throat would be, how ashamed you would feel—and then you left the kitchen and went straight upstairs to your bedroom, shut the door, and began your deep breathing exercises? Is that right?"

2. Ask the client to summarize and repeat the changes ("Now, tell me again, what is it that helped you the most yesterday when you had this urge to binge. Tell me what you specifically did differently").

3. Compliment the client and support her efforts ("I am really impressed with these changes you have made. They are significant. You have really worked hard and should be very proud of yourself"). Such reinforcement can be done two or three times throughout the session.

Maintenance/Relapse Stage

The final stage of change is referred to as the maintenance stage. In the maintenance stage, the client

- Reports consistent progress
- Is able to identify relapse prevention behaviors

The therapist

- Identifies possible obstacles to continued success
- Amplifies, reinforces, and highlights changes
- Helps the client develop her relapse plan
- Works to keep the door open for further assistance

The therapist must reinforce the specific actions and interactions that are maintaining the behavior change. Miller (1989) says, "Maintenance is the real challenge in all of the addictive behaviors" (p. 70), and this is especially true of eating disorders, since relapse is very common. Continuing to focus on how the client is able to maintain the changes and prevent relapse can often yield a variety of strategies not previously identified. And according to Miller & Rollnick (1991), maintaining the change may require different strategies or skills than those that initiated the change in the first place.

Thus, it is helpful to plan for relapse and establish an action plan that contains the client's solution patterns as the keys to getting the client back on track. This planning should be discussed openly with the client:

THERAPIST: [Sara], you have made significant progress. I am really impressed with the amount of hard work you have demonstrated these past six weeks.

CLIENT: Gee, thanks.

THERAPIST: Given your progress, you are now at a point where you are ready to take the next and final step in therapy as we prepare to terminate. You need to develop a relapse plan as a preventive measure.

CLIENT: Yeah, I know. That's what scares me. Although I've never been able to stay abstinent this long, I worry about relapsing.

THERAPIST: Well, you definitely need to think about it, so you can rebuild your chain of success as quickly as possible.

CLIENT: In the past when I would go off and binge and purge, I would just freak out and then think, "Aw, what the hell. What damn difference does it make. I am so damn weak, I might as well as go ahead and eat some more. Who gives a shit." And I'd be off to the races again.

THERAPIST: So let's take a look at specifically what you will do differently if, in fact, you should break the chain.

Working closely with the client in establishing a preventive plan is the last step in the process, and it must be done painstakingly, with specific details discussed. At EDRC, clients are asked to write out their plans.

During the action stage, the therapist must work diligently to normalize the potential relapse and help the client recognize that the pattern of problem behavior, given its biobehavioral components, is going to take much continued patience, persistence, and hard work to change. The therapist's task is to encourage the client and renew her determination to get back on track if she does falter.

These models of relationship types and of stages of change contain the critical elements needed to promote change and efficiency within the therapeutic process. By being sensitive to the client's stage of change, continuously assessing the therapeutic relationship, and working to identify what difference the client specifically wants to see as a result of therapy, clinicians who treat eating disorder clients can strengthen the therapeutic alliance and promote extremely high levels of cooperation.

In the next two chapters, I will describe in detail the solution-focused interviewing strategies of the first and subsequent sessions. I will also explore specific homework tasks for clients.

Five

The First Sessions:
Key Interviewing Questions

Alice knew it was the Rabbit coming to look for her,
and she trembled till she shook the house, quite
forgetting that she was now about a thousand times
as large as the Rabbit, and had no reason to be
afraid of it.

—*Lewis Carroll*
Alice's Adventures in Wonderland

There can be no doubt that the first session in treatment is the most critical, as it sets the tone for every subsequent session. Moreover, given the eating disorder client's proclivity for fixating on her *disorder*, it is crucial that this first session be structured to focus on finding a *solution*.

Interviewing for Presession Change and
Previous Treatment Gains

The solution-focused model adheres to the belief that change occurs constantly. In their research, the team at the Brief Family Therapy Center discovered that many clients identified changes in their problem situation between the time they first made the appointment for therapy and the actual visit (Weiner-Davis, deShazer, & Gingerich, 1987). Other research also supports the presence of presession change (Bloom, 1981; Noonan, 1973; Talmon, 1990). Because they tend to be obsessive and to have cognitive distortions related to perfectionist and dichotomous thinking, many eating disorder clients are deeply entrenched in their binge and purge

behaviors and unaware of any positive changes that might be occurring in those behaviors. However, as the Sims and Milan family
cases cited in Chapter Three illustrate, there are clear benefits in
assessing clients for presession change.

It is also vital for the therapist to know whether the individual
with an eating disorder has had previous therapy, and if so, how
much, what kind, and how it was helpful. In research at EDRC, I
have found that the majority of my clients have previously engaged
in either some form of inpatient and/or outpatient therapy or a
twelve-step support group, such as Overeaters Anonymous. However, my purpose in exploring previous treatment history is radically
different from the purpose of such explorations in traditional therapy. My solution-focused goal is to assess *what's been better* as a result
of treatment. Questions that focus on previous therapy include:

• *What kind and type of therapy did you have in treating your eating
   disorder?*

Answers to this question should give the therapist an idea of
whether the client has had inpatient or outpatient treatment or
individual or group therapy. A history of participation in a structured treatment program is a fairly strong indicator that the eating
disorder client has received considerable individual, group, and family therapy, and that she has participated in psychoeducational
groups, body image groups, nutritional counseling, and aftercare.
Consequently, this client has a tremendous knowledge base. She
probably knows the specifics of her eating disorder and has a heightened level of understanding regarding herself and the dynamics of
her interpersonal relational style. The therapist spends only a few
minutes on this question, just long enough to gather the facts of the
client's clinical treatment résumé. As discussed later in this chapter, this information will be used at key points in the interview to
emphasize client resources and strengths.

- *Was your treatment helpful and if so, how was it helpful?*

Our research has demonstrated that the vast majority of clients report that their therapy was helpful, even if they terminated prematurely or dropped out. However, if they disliked their therapist or felt their therapist did not understand their problem, they were more likely to report their therapy was not helpful at all.

The therapist does not take much time for the first part of this question, but spends considerably more time on the issue of how the therapy was helpful, if it was. At this point, the therapist and client can review what has been better as a result of the client's previous treatment and specifically how her eating or purging behaviors have gotten better (as is illustrated in the following conversation).

THERAPIST: So you were on an inpatient unit for two months, and you stopped using laxatives altogether and stopped purging as well? For about six months after you got out? Is that right?

CLIENT: Yeah.

THERAPIST: So for six months after you were discharged, you were able to abstain from laxatives and purging? Wow! You really used that intensive therapy well. How did you do that?

CLIENT: Yeah. Well, not quite six months, maybe more like four or five. But so what, things have gotten just as bad as they were before I went into the hospital. Actually, they might even be worse.

THERAPIST: Yeah. So tell me how you were able to abstain during those four or five months?

CLIENT: Well, it was just better then; I mean, I don't really know.

THERAPIST: What was it about your therapy that helped you the most? Four or five months is a really long time. You must have been doing something different then.

CLIENT: Well, . . . now that you ask, I was keeping a journal of my feelings and sharing them in aftercare. I stopped doing both, and things went downhill. I'm throwing up about four or five times a day now and using laxatives, maybe not as much as before, but I'm still using them.

THERAPIST: So tell me how keeping a journal of your feelings and sharing them in aftercare was helpful to you during that time?

By focusing on the details of her abstinence rather than her current symptoms, this line of questioning supports the client's previous treatment experiences and acknowledges her efforts and hard work in taking responsibility for her problem. It also can give the therapist and client useful information about previous solution patterns.

Questions to Amplify and Highlight Benefits of Therapy

Once the client and therapist discuss changes that have occurred as a result of therapy, the therapist then explores these changes by focusing on specific details of who, what, where, why, and when. An example is the continuing conversation in the previous interview, as the client answers the therapist's question about the helpfulness of the client's journal writing.

CLIENT: Well, I don't know. I mean, I guess it helped me open up more to myself.

THERAPIST: Sounds like you worked hard at journaling and going to those meetings. That really takes a lot of commitment. So, how was that helpful? Opening yourself up more to yourself.

CLIENT: Well, see, I have this problem with anger. I tend to keep it stuffed inside, and what I learned on the unit was that if I opened up more and expressed it I wouldn't feel the

urge to abuse myself. Writing it down and then talking
about it in the group kept me more in touch with my anger.

THERAPIST: So when you had this urge to abuse yourself, what
did you do that was helpful? That helped you control the
urge?

CLIENT: I don't know . . . I mean, I never thought about it.
[*Pauses.*] Well, when I had the urge I would pull out my
journal . . . I carried it around with me all of the time . . .
and I would write down my feelings, . . . usually it was
always feelings of anger.

THERAPIST: So when you had the urge to abuse yourself, you
would pull out your journal and write down your feelings?
Is that right? When would you do this?

CLIENT: Yeah. I always wrote in my journal at night and
reviewed what significant feelings I had during that day. But
you know, if I had the urge to take a laxative, even at work,
I would take out my journal and write down what I was
feeling. That seemed to work then.

THERAPIST: Well, how do you suppose writing in your journal
might be helpful now?

It is important to find out if the client believes previous solutions can continue to be helpful. The therapist also needs to
emphasize how much hard work the client has done in her previous therapy. This technique is particularly useful in working
with eating disorder clients, since they often do not acknowledge
their accomplishments, yet at the same time they tend to be high
achievers. Treating their high need for achievement and the tendency to work especially hard at achieving as a resource, the therapist can emphasize the accomplishments the client has achieved
as a result of therapy.

As mentioned earlier, eating disorder clients also have a tendency toward magical thinking: they believe something outside of
themselves will fix them and this fix will happen quickly. As long

as they view themselves as inherently deficient, only a miracle can possibly save them from their plight. Many clients believe this miracle will result if they could only understand the underlying causes of their problem behaviors. Consequently, they have some vague notion that an exploration of some aspect of their past, undertaken with the judgment and guidance of a therapist or some self-help book, will provide the key to their cure. However, in my clinical experience, a focus on underlying causes does very little to empower the client to recognize her competencies and internal resources. It does even less to help the client face the reality that changes in her binging, purging, or restricting will take patience, persistence, and hard work. Much like the binge and purge syndrome itself, in which the client wishes to eat her cake and have it too, is the notion often promoted in traditional therapy that the magic of effective change will grow out of some mystical experience in the therapist's office rather than out of specific client actions. Effective therapy must focus the client on what she is specifically *doing* that makes a difference in her problem eating and restricting behaviors. She must heighten her awareness of her own idiosyncratic pathways to the achievement of her goal. And this focus can empower her and increase her sense of personal efficacy.

The Magic of Miracles

The most fundamental clinical question of the solution-focused model is known as the *miracle question*. Derived from Erickson's crystal ball technique (1954a), which was developed to project the client into a future that was successful, the miracle question similarly asks the client to imagine what life would be like without her complaint. In responding to this question, the client actually constructs her own solution, which then guides the therapeutic process. Berg and Miller (1992) describe this phrasing for the miracle question: "I want to ask you a slightly different question now. You will have to use your imagination for this one. Suppose you go home and go to bed tonight after today's session. While you are sleeping a miracle happens and the problem that brought you here is solved, just like that (snapping a finger). Since you were sleeping, you didn't know that this miracle happened. What do you suppose will be the first small thing that will indicate to you tomorrow morning that there has been a miracle overnight and the problem that brought you here is solved?" (p. 78).

According to deShazer (1988), this question is a powerful frame for helping clients establish goals. As they describe what life will be like when the problem is solved, they are helped to build the expectation that there is a solution to the problem and to actually believe and behave in ways that will lead to fulfilling this expectation. My clinical experience with this question, which supports Berg and Miller's and deShazer's, is that clients are extremely realistic and cooperative in detailing the morning after the miracle. In contrast to probing for a history of the complaint, the therapist who asks this question assesses the client's current situation and her picture of the future. Consequently, at EDRC, therapy cannot begin until we have first gained an understanding of the client's miracle picture. As deShazer notes (1988), when the description of the future includes a continuance of exceptions related to the complaint, then the therapist can be more assured that she or he is moving in the right direction.

Here is the response to the miracle question of a client who identified herself as bulimic and as binging and purging two to three times a day. This is what she saw happening on her miracle day.

CLIENT: I wouldn't have a craving. Then I would not, as soon as I woke up, be thinking of what I was going to have for breakfast.
THERAPIST: So what would you be thinking about instead?
CLIENT: What I'm going to do. Things I'm going to get done. I'd look forward to that day instead of dreading it.
THERAPIST: What else?

CLIENT: I would be eating the right kinds of foods and wanting to do so. I'd have a bagel and juice for breakfast and a salad and my fat-free dressing on it for lunch. I'd be going to exercise and excited about it. This is the way I used to be. [*This spontaneous statement of an exception was explored later in the interview.*]

THERAPIST: Who would be the first to notice that this miracle had happened?

CLIENT: My husband.

THERAPIST: So what would he notice different about you on this day?

CLIENT: Well, first of all, he'd notice that I lost twenty pounds!

THERAPIST: So how would you be different then?

CLIENT: I'd have this whole new attitude. I'd be happier about myself. You know my husband is really disappointed in me. . . . because I sit around the house a lot more and watch too much television. I don't go out much or dress up like I used to.

THERAPIST: So on miracle day, how could he tell that you had this whole new attitude and that you were happy about yourself?

CLIENT: He'd see me out of the house! Going to the gym every morning. Calling friends up and asking them to do things.

THERAPIST: So when he sees you out of the house, going to the gym, and calling up friends, how might he be different on miracle day?

CLIENT: He'd be happier. He gets so down when I'm down. He probably wouldn't be so withdrawn and tense.

In this interview, I expanded on this client's miracle day for thirty minutes, probing how the client would be different. Goals were formulated both from the client's response to the miracle question and the spontaneous exception she identified. In this case, the client decided to go to the fitness club in her area first, to see how much it cost. Since she was so self-conscious about her weight gain, she was not encouraged to sign up but rather just to explore if she might feel comfortable using this particular place as her gym. By her third session, she had purchased a club membership, and by the fifth session, she was working out regularly and had reduced her binging and purging significantly.

In the EDRC group program (detailed in Chapter Seven), the miracle question is also used in developing the client's treatment plan and is modified and adapted throughout treatment to help keep the client and therapist focused on the client's goals for therapy. Every client answers the miracle question in writing, along with other related questions, at the time of the assessment. Here is a typical written answer to the miracle question.

> My miracle day would begin with me waking up thinner! I don't mean extremely thin or body gorgeous. I mean healthy. Appropriate weight for my size frame, build at 150 lbs. I would have no hang up about my body—it would be the least priority instead of always my first priority. My actions would include activities that are very active, swimming, softball, etc. My family and friends would not be concerned with how I look (body wise). I guess my miracle day is when my body is not a priority on how it looks in and out of clothes and when I can just relate to people—family and co-workers without my body image getting in the way. I would feel freer—more outgoing—less intimidated if my body were in better shape. Food would not be a priority. . . . [Who would be the first to notice?] My husband would notice that I am more willing to do activities that he knows I like. He would also notice that I would be more outgoing and happier.

In the assessment interview, the written response is fleshed out, exceptions are explored, and the client identifies specifically what she wants to be different as a result of treatment. Preliminary treatment goals are established from this database. Initial treatment goals for the client who wanted to wake up thinner included developing a food plan that incorporated the food pyramid (the required food groups), increasing physical activity by first researching local YMCAs and their swimming facilities (the client had identified an exception that occurred when she was swimming three times a week and felt that food was less of a priority and her body was in better shape), and increasing positive feelings toward her body by participating in the EDRC body image groups.

However, if the client's response does not include any exceptions related to dietary practices or purging activities, then, as the interview progresses and the miracle picture is fleshed out, the therapist specifically asks the client how her problematic eating or restricting behavior will be different. The therapist incorporates the client's idiosyncratic descriptor of the problematic behavior into the question, saying, for example: "How will your 'obsession with food' be different on this miracle day?"

This focusing is often necessary, since many clients do not spontaneously describe how the eating disorder itself would be different on this day. The response to the focused question is the one that will help the client and therapist explore realistic solutions. Client and therapist can then work to negotiate a goal that is meaningful to the client, and most of all, one that is realistic and achievable. Examining our taped interviews, my colleagues and I at EDRC discovered that if we did not focus the client by discussing how her eating would be different on Miracle Day and if we then negotiated an unrelated goal, which she may in fact have achieved, she would simply return to her initial focus of wanting to be "rid of" her eating disorder.

The Ripple Effect

In the two cases just described, the goals codeveloped by the client and therapist specifically addressed eating or exercise behaviors. There are times, however, when the negotiated goal may seem completely unrelated to the eating disorder and yet create a ripple effect that alters that problem behavior. Such a ripple effect occurred from the following conversation.

THERAPIST: So last weekend was the most recent time you remember when you didn't binge or purge at all?

CLIENT: Yes. Last weekend. Not once; but of course, I've been binging and purging my brains out ever since.

THERAPIST: Hm. So, the entire weekend, all of Saturday and Sunday?

CLIENT: Well, actually, even though I binged and purged on Friday afternoon, I didn't Friday evening.

THERAPIST: Wow, that's quite an accomplishment. So what was different this past weekend that you were able to do that?

CLIENT: Well, I don't know. I was busier this past weekend. I called one of the people I know at work and asked her if she wanted to go shopping. So we did and then went to dinner and a movie.

THERAPIST: That's different for you? To call someone up and ask them to do something?

CLIENT: Yeah. Really different. I really don't feel comfortable with anyone here yet. I've only been here for a few months.

THERAPIST: So how did you decide to go ahead and call this person?

CLIENT: Well, I just decided that I was sick and tired of being sick and tired. I mean my throat hurts so bad, I just decided what the hell. So I just picked up the phone and called Jill to see if she wanted to go shopping. To my surprise, she was really happy to hear from me, and we had a great day.

THERAPIST: That's great. So tell me how this helped you as far as your binging and purging goes.

CLIENT: Well, . . . I guess being with someone really helps. It just makes me feel less lonely. I mean I really had a good close circle of friends back home, and we did lots of things together, but that's all changed now that I've moved. I don't know anyone here.

THERAPIST: Except for Jill, I guess.

CLIENT [*laughing*]: Yeah, except for Jill!

THERAPIST: So tell me what you have to do to have more weekends like this past one. Where you didn't binge or purge at all.

CLIENT: Well, I guess it helps to be busy. But it's more than that. For me, it really helps to have a friend. My binging and purging really got much worse when I moved here. I didn't know anybody when I took this job. I guess what helps is having a friend. Someone you can talk to and do things with.

In this situation, the conversation began to shift from a focus on the eating behaviors to an exception that involved socialization. Eventually, the client agreed that she needed to develop more social relationships, and this became her negotiated goal. Two subsequent sessions encouraged her to maintain the changes she made toward reaching this goal. The changes had a positive impact on her eating behaviors, and therapy terminated.

Because eating disorder clients generally have vague and unrealistic expectations of therapy, wanting nothing less than being completely rid of their problem, a patient and careful exploration of the miracle question generates not only a sense of hopefulness and a more realistic view of the future in these clients, but also places the responsibility for change directly on them.

Exploration of Exceptions

Once the miracle picture is fleshed out, the therapist then uses it as a launch point to explore exceptions. Thus, at this point in the interview, the therapist and client specifically and painstakingly detail the exceptions they can find, as illustrated in the following conversation. Note that the therapist bases the first question on the supposition that the client has in fact experienced a day like the miracle day she described. Using such suppositional language is imperative. If the therapist phrases the question more tentatively and asks, "Have you ever had a day like the one you just described?" the client is likely to respond, "Never".

THERAPIST: When most recently have you had a day like this or anything close to it?

CLIENT: I guess when I was on vacation with my husband. Just two weeks ago. We had a great time.

THERAPIST: So which particular day came closest to the miracle day you just described?

CLIENT: It would have been on a Friday. The day after we arrived.

THERAPIST: So tell me. What was different on that day that made it most like a miracle day?

CLIENT: We got up early that morning and took a walk down the beach. I was so relaxed and felt so happy. Actually, we first had breakfast, and I had a really healthy one. Some fat-free yogurt with this fabulous fresh fruit, a bagel with fat-free cream cheese, and coffee.

THERAPIST: Is that different? For you to have a really healthy breakfast like that?

CLIENT: Oh gosh, yes. I usually don't eat breakfast at all.

As the client and therapist continued to explore this exception related to the client's miracle day and other exceptions, they discovered that having breakfast made a difference in the client's eating behaviors for the remainder of her day, and the client recognized that this difference was the direct result of her own decision to eat a "healthy breakfast."

Oftentimes, clients will spontaneously talk about exceptions.

THERAPIST: So you will be more confident on Miracle Day? What else?

CLIENT: Yeah, more confident. I'd really be like my old self.

THERAPIST: So tell me more about what your old self is like.

In this case, I explored more specifically what the client was like as her "old self" and, later in the interview, probed for details to find out when the client most recently was like her old self.

If no exceptions are noted, then the therapist helps the client project success into the future (Berg & Miller, 1992). At EDRC, we simply ask the client to pretend she had a day close to her miracle day and to describe what this simulated exception looks like.

DeShazer (1988) distinguishes two types of exceptions: *random* or *spontaneous exceptions* are those that the client views as flukes or chance events; *deliberate exceptions* are those that the client sees resulting from a deliberate shift in behavior. But on their own, clients do not find either of these types significant for the potential solution of their complaint (deShazer, 1988). Given their proclivity toward perfectionistic, dichotomous thinking, eating disorder clients are prone to discount or minimize the value of these exceptions. They discount *all* the exceptions. Therefore, therapists must be particularly cautious not to emphasize an exception in a way that may lead the client to believe the therapist is patronizing her or does not understand the seriousness of her complaint. Rather than debate whether or not an exception is meaningful, it is more useful for the therapist to exhibit puzzlement or confusion at the client's dismissal of it.

THERAPIST: So are you saying that for the past two days, instead of taking your usual six or eight laxatives before you went to bed, you only took two? How did you do that?

CLIENT: Yeah. But so what! I am still taking them, and I hate myself for being so weak. It's so disgusting.

THERAPIST: Knowing that you have been taking lots and lots of laxatives before bedtime for such a long time, I am still puzzled as to how you managed to only take two.

This line of questioning, which highlights success or small steps of success, influences the client's perceptions of self-efficacy in a very positive way. As Miller (1992a) notes, "By asking how a client has been able to make some progress, or to maintain or prevent . . . problems from becoming worse, the therapist and client are able to review situations that appeared to be failures as solutions that simply went unnoticed" (p. 7).

The Magic of Numbers

Once an exception is explored fully, the therapist can begin to negotiate goals with the client. A specific interview technique that helps in the negotiating process is the scaling question. According to deShazer and Berg (1993), scaling questions are a means of allowing the client and therapist to jointly construct a manner of talking about things that would otherwise be difficult to describe: "scales allow both therapist and client to use the way language works naturally by agreeing upon terms (i.e., numbers) and a concept (a scale where 10 stands for the goal and zero stands for an absence of progress toward that goal) that is obviously multiple and flexible" (p. 19).

In the first session, I can use a scaling question to establishing treatment goals, as the therapist did with the client described earlier whose exception occurred while she was on vacation with her spouse.

THERAPIST: So on a scale of 0 to 10, with 10 being the miracle day you just described and 0 being the farthest from it, where does your vacation with your husband fall?

CLIENT: Oh, I'd say about an 8.

THERAPIST: That's great! Where do you fall today on that same scale?

CLIENT: About a 5.

THERAPIST: So what do you suppose will have to happen in order for you to move up one level on that scale . . . to a 6?

In addition, once a goal is established in the first session, the therapist can also use a scale to determine client motivation. For example, with this same client I asked, "Now on another scale, with 10 being you are very likely to purchase healthy breakfast food and 0 being highly unlikely, where do you fall on that scale today?"

Establishment of Proximal Goals

Realistic and achievable goals should emerge from these conversations geared toward deconstructing or dissolving the complaint. Well-formed and efficient goals are the foundation of the solution-focused model since they are guideposts for both therapist and client to determine treatment progress and termination. However, goals must be developed to match the dominant type of client-therapist relationship (Berg & Miller, 1992). Moreover, according to Miller (1993), goals must be

- Salient to the client
- Described in situational and contextual terms
- Described in interactional and interpersonal terms
- Described as the "presence of something" rather than the "absence of something"
- Realistic and achievable within the context of the client's life

Although eating disorder clients' desire to be totally free of their complaint is an acceptable distal goal, it is too grandiose to be a workable initial goal. Therefore, establishing and reinforcing prox-imal subgoals related to eating behaviors is an essential aspect of treatment. Clients must be encouraged to identify small and realis-tic steps toward achieving their goals.

THERAPIST: So what is it you have to do in order to move up one level on the scale?

CLIENT: Well, I'd have to stop binging when I come home from work.

THERAPIST: That sounds more like three steps up! What has to happen in order for you to move up just one, just one level on the scale?

CLIENT: Just one, huh? Well, I guess I'd have to maybe start eating lunch. When I eat lunch, I'm less likely to binge when I get home from work.

THERAPIST: So what has to be different so that you would start eating lunch?

CLIENT: Well, I know that if I go out for lunch that won't help, because I tend to overeat when I do that. But when I bring my lunch to work and eat at my desk, I usually eat some-thing that's good for me, and that really helps me 'cause I'm not as hungry when I get home. Plus, I really feel good about myself since I ate so well at lunch.

THERAPIST: So what has to happen in order for you to move up one level on the scale?

CLIENT: I'd have to bring my lunch to work.

THERAPIST: And so what has to be different so that you could start bringing your lunch to work?

CLIENT: Well, I'd have to go to the store and get the stuff I need for salads. I know how to make really good low-cal salads.

In this session, I concentrated on helping the client develop a small proximal subgoal related to her distal goal of wanting to stop binging. This negotiation process requires patience and persistence to keep the client focused on the small steps needed to achieve her larger goal. The therapist also needs to remind the client of the importance of taking small steps in managing her problem behaviors, otherwise, the client will minimize or discount her gains just because they are small.

Given the negative physiological consequences of eating disorders, many clinicians tend to take it upon themselves to determine the goals of therapy. This will typically result in resistance and a general lack of cooperation, particularly if the client-therapist relationship is a visitor- or complainant-type relationship. Therefore, I emphasize again that the first step in therapy should be to find out what the client wants and then to negotiate goals that are salient to the client. In my experience with eating disorder clients, treatment proceeds much more smoothly when I start where the client is.

In her workshops, Insoo Kim Berg has underscored the client's need to perceive any goal as requiring hard work. I find this stance to be particularly useful with eating disorder clients. Whatever goal is negotiated, the therapist must emphasize that success will require a strong effort on the part of the client. By the same token, when a goal is achieved, the therapist needs to acknowledge the hard work the client has completed. Conversely, if a goal is not met, the therapist needs to indicate that the client will have to work harder. By accentuating the hard work involved, the therapist helps the client feel less like a failure during the time she fails to achieve her goal even though she is proceeding toward it. This is perhaps one of the most important aspects of goal formulation for eating disorder clients who engage in the magical thinking that says their eating disorder should disappear simply because they are in therapy. The therapist's emphasis on the client's work encourages the client to develop a more realistic stance regarding goal completion. In addition, the client is in a better position to decide if she really wants to invest that much energy into her treatment.

Putting It All Together: First Session

Given that the first session sets the tone for the remainder of therapy and predisposes the client to function in either a problem-focused groove or a solution-focused groove, it is by far the most critical session in the treatment process. This section describes the progress of that session in detail. One initial overall suggestion is that the therapist pretend that the first session may very well be the last session she will have with the client (a strategy put forward by Lynn Johnson [personal communication, July 1994]). Adopting this mindset compels the therapist not only to be as efficient as possible but also to ensure that the client leaves the session with something constructive.

The first session can be divided into three phases. The first, or beginning, phase generally lasts about five to seven minutes. Here, the client tells her story. A review of taped EDRC sessions shows that it is during this storytelling process that the client often identifies her core objective for seeking counseling, an objective that will emerge repeatedly throughout her therapy. The therapist must note the exact words used by the client to describe this core objective. Two examples of client expressions of core objectives are, "I just need to get control of my eating," and, "I have to break this habit and start eating normally again."

Depending upon the flow of the session, presession change and/or previous treatment gains can also be explored in the first phase.

During the second, or middle, phase, the therapist needs to project the client into an alternate reality and ask the miracle question. This aspect of the middle phase lasts anywhere from ten to thirty minutes depending upon how much the therapist probes.

According to deShazer (1988), getting the client to describe a future in which the problem is solved achieves two objectives. First, it builds the client's expectation that the problem is solvable. Once this expectation, or prophecy of success, is formed, the client is more likely to think and behave in ways that lead to fulfilling the prophecy (deShazer, 1988). Second, although clients want to be rid of their problem eating, restricting, or purging behaviors, they generally have no idea what the replacement for these problem patterns might be. An exploration of a miracle day helps clients formulate what these specific replacements might be.

Once the miracle picture is fleshed out by exploring who, what, where, and when, the therapist then searches for exceptions—that is, those times when the miracle is already happening, if only just a little bit—carefully investigating what is different during these exceptional times, and cooperating with the client to identify a goal as a result of this investigation. Through this technique, the client constructs her own solution based on her unique resources, previous solution patterns, and preceding successes.

The third, or ending, phase of the first session lasts approximately four to five minutes. Once the client and therapist have explored exceptions, the therapist takes a break in order to consult with the treatment team (deShazer, 1985) or to reflect alone on the course of the interview. The therapist assesses the client's stage of change and type of therapeutic relationship (according to the characteristics described earlier), formulates a feedback message, and if appropriate, designs a homework task (Miller, 1992b).

Feedback Messages

A feedback message has four parts (Miller, 1993).

1. Compliments that highlight specific positive or helpful client actions in order to help the client frame her situation differently ("The goal is to help clients see themselves as normal persons with normal difficulties," [deShazer et al., 1986, p. 216]).
2. An agreement with and a restatement of the client's goal in seeking counseling, using the client's language.

3. A rationale for the homework given.
4. The actual homework task.

In the following example of an actual feedback message, client language is indicated by quotation marks.

> [Sharon], first of all I would like to compliment you on your decision to begin working on "controlling your weight in healthier, more normal ways." Based on what you told me, as a result of the hard work you put into your previous therapy, you have already been able to totally stop using laxatives by increasing your running from twelve miles a week to fifteen miles a week. This seems to make a big difference. However, I do agree with you it certainly is not enough. Your "inability" to "control" your "compulsive binging" is what needs to be "resolved".
>
> Since you want to "focus on this issue of resolving your compulsive binging," I am going to ask you if you would be willing to do something between now and the next time we meet.

Solution-Focused Homework Tasks

Once the feedback message is constructed, the therapist must decide on a homework task, or intervention. Therapeutic tasks and directives are particularly significant in solution-oriented models because the client is expected to actively participate in the process. Instead of being something magical that is done *to* clients, therapy becomes something that requires client effort and work, and clients are expected to complete therapeutic activities between sessions. Such interventions are a significant means of increasing clients' perceptions of self-efficacy and promoting client change. However, in assigning tasks, therapists must heed these three points.

• The therapist must assess the type of therapeutic relationship and/or the client's stage of change before assigning a directive (Berg & Miller, 1992).

Precontemplators (visitor relationships) do not receive a task since these clients do not believe there is a problem.

Contemplators (complainant relationships) are given an observational task in an attempt to alter their view of the problem situation.

Actors (customer relationships) are given a doing task, since they see themselves as a part of the solution.

• When feasible, existing exceptions to the problem are integrated into the task. Since most clients have rigid mindsets and are not aware of their self-formulated solutions, these homework tasks can reconfigure the client's awareness that the exceptions to their problem behaviors are indeed different and significant.

• In delivering a therapeutic task to the client, the therapist must explain its purpose (Miller, 1992b). If the client perceives the task as salient and meaningful to her situation, she will be more likely to carry it out.

The two following homework tasks are typically assigned in the first session and have proven to be useful in working with eating disorder clients. Because of the integral part these tasks play in the therapeutic process, treatment sessions are typically scheduled two to three weeks apart in order to allow sufficient time for change to occur as a result of the tasks (and to promote less client dependence on therapy).

Coin Toss. This solution-focused task is intended to make the client's random exceptions more deliberate. Miller (1993) describes the way the therapist assigns this task: "Between now and our next session, I am going to ask you to take a quarter . . . and place it on your nightstand. [When you arise], I want you to toss the coin . . . if it comes up 'heads' you are to pretend you are having a Miracle Day. If it comes up 'tails,' I want you to have a regular day. However, on the days it comes up heads, note what is different on those days and then report your observations to me at our next session."

The following conversation took place at the second session for a client who was a compulsive eater and had been given the coin toss as a homework task.

THERAPIST: So tell me what's better since we last met?

CLIENT: Well, um, today is probably not so better but what happened . . . when I left here last week is . . . well . . . it doesn't take me long to put two and two together. I know that I don't have to use the flip of a coin to empower myself so I had left here at first planning to go have this really big lunch—then I thought, "Well, I don't have to do that!" And so I didn't! [*Laughs.*]

THERAPIST: So what did you do instead?

CLIENT: I had this pretty decent lunch. It was a choice . . . my choice. That was one of those things I realized after I left here. That I had a choice.

THERAPIST: Really? That's great.

CLIENT: On the way home from lunch, I could [have gone] home and isolate[d]—which I do a lot of the time, but instead, I stopped by and saw a friend for a few hours and we talked and talked and we just couldn't talk fast enough!

In this case, the client began to make changes without even doing the task! Other clients have often returned having made significant changes as a result of the coin toss. However, these changes can go unnoticed unless the therapist continues to ask questions that point up the changes.

In one case, a client reported at the second session that she had gotten tails (regular days) three days in a row. At which time, she threw the coin on the floor and decided that she was going to have a miracle day no matter what! In another case, the client had four days of heads (miracle days) and was reticent to toss the coin on the fifth day. She realized that although she had really good days, it took a lot of hard work on her part to make these miracle days happen. She decided to have a tails day without taking the chance of tossing the coin so she could just take a rest!

To give the client a task variation that gives her more control over the outcome, the therapist can ask her to predict the night before whether or not she will have a miracle day upon arising and then to note what is different on those days.

In EDRC's group treatment program, the coin toss is used as a task at two different points in treatment. Clients receive copies of the responses they wrote to the miracle day question at the time of intake. In the group, they are instructed to review that response and alter it in any way they wish. After they have been given sufficient time to complete this task, their group discussion centers around these two questions: "When is this miracle day, or a piece of the miracle day, already happening? and, What is different about those times?

Through sharing their individual miracle days and focusing on when and how they are already occurring, group members help each other expand and clarify the exceptions they uncover. At the end of the group session, the coin toss assignment is given with these instructions:

- Pay attention to how you feel different on a miracle day.
- Pay attention to what others notice that is different about you on a miracle day.

In the follow-up session which usually takes place two weeks later, the miracle day responses are redistributed, and clients are asked to share their observations from the past two weeks, focusing on what was different and what worked.

The objective of the group processing is to help group members establish as clearly as possible what is different on miracle days, what specifically they did to make these days happen, and what they need to do to continue having such days. Through group discussion and support, members have the opportunity to develop specific information regarding their actions and choices, and this promotes the occurrence of more miracle days.

As would be expected, group members in the action stage of change are most likely to actually do the task and discuss the results. Members in the contemplation stage generally do not do the task, or they alter it to make it more acceptable. For example, one group member, after having done the task for a few days, made the decision that each time the coin turned up heads she would pretend it was tails. She indicated that trying to have a miracle day imposed too much pressure on her. Yet through group processing, much to her surprise, she became aware of things she actually did do differently during the two weeks, even though she had not done the task as assigned.

One particular advantage of assigning this task in group programs is that group members have the opportunity to observe in the experiences of others as well as their own experiences what could work and what could be different if they chose to take action.

Observation. When the therapist has assessed that the client is in the contemplation stage of change and a complainant therapeutic relationship, she or he formulates an observation task related to the client's stated reason for seeking counseling.

For example, the therapist might ask the client to pay close attention to the times she has the urge to binge, purge, or restrict but does *not*. The client is instructed to return to the next session with a detailed report of what is different about those times. Or the therapist might ask the client to pay attention to those times she feels "resolved" about her eating disorder, even if only a little bit. The observation task must be phrased to include the client's idiosyncratic expression of what it is she wants to be different. For example, a client who wants to be "more in control" of her eating might be asked to, "Pay attention to the times you feel 'more in control' of your eating"; while the client who wants her behavior to be "more normal" might be asked to, "Pay attention to the times that your eating is 'more normal.'"

First Session Focus

Through the use of specific interviewing questions, the solution-focused model continually works on orienting the client toward change as well as on establishing salient goals and subgoals. The first session focuses on

- Attending to the present and the future, with very little attention paid to the problem or the past
- Exploring a problem-free future
- Examining exceptions and previous solution patterns
- Jointly creating reality based on the client's truth and seeking to understand the client's language
- Providing feedback and therapeutic compliments
- Assigning homework tasks based on the client-therapist relationship and client stage of change

Second Session and Beyond

The second session provides the therapist with significant information regarding the client's stage of change. Second sessions *always* begin with the question, "What's better since our last session?" (Miller, 1992b) or "What have you done right for yourself?" (L. Johnson, personal communication, 1994).

If the client launches into solution talk and focuses on those things that are better, the therapist's job is to highlight and amplify the changed behavior and direct the client to "do more of it!" (rule 2 of the solution-focused model). After asking scaling questions about client confidence, a technique that helps both client and therapist assess for the likelihood of ongoing success, the therapist needs to probe whether these changes are enough. That is, wheth... the client is now satisfied with the goals achieved and can begin to disengage from therapy.

Many clients at this stage wish to build their confidence in their ability to sustain their new behaviors, and they spontaneously request maintenance therapy, with appointments set up monthly or every six weeks and the understanding that the client who feels she needs to touch base sooner can always call for an interim appointment. (Our experience at EDRC has demonstrated that clients maintain for three to five sessions, over several months, and then terminate.)

At the outset of the second session the client may indicate that nothing is better. It is important not to take this declaration at face value, since these clients have a propensity for focusing on those things that did not go well. In our experience, a persistent and careful exploration of the events between the first and second session frequently results in the client's reporting exceptions, much to her surprise! If the client persists in the vein that nothing is better, the therapist then needs to explore what kept her from getting worse. This too can highlight possible exceptions and maintain a framework of solutions and exceptions.

At this point in the interview, it is critical for the therapist to

- Separate the person from the problem. Stay focused on the client's strengths and resources.
- *Not* take a position regarding the client's situation. Refrain from speculating about the client or making assumptions related to the lack of progress.
- Check if the client's goal is the same or if it has changed. Begin to discuss specifically what difference the client wants to see as a result of therapy. If the client's goal seems to have changed, share this observation with the client.
- Evaluate the client's stage of change more carefully.

The interview should focus on the mutual negotiation of a solvable complaint. During the middle phase of the second session, it is often helpful to have the client complete the circle of influence task (see Chapter Six), which can show both therapist and client what the client perceives her level of control to be in solving the complaint. This knowledge can shift the conversation to what is really possible.

The end phase of the second session is similar to the end of the first. The therapist takes a break and formulates the feedback message and homework task based on an assessment of the client's stage of change and relationship type.

Along with a continued focus on solutions and goals, three key issues generally infuse therapeutic conversations in subsequent sessions.

- The necessity of the client's taking small steps to ameliorate the problem eating and purging behaviors
- The necessity of the client's developing realistic expectations for herself in the light of the negative physiological results of her repeated dieting and restricting or binging and purging
- The necessity of the client's learning to tolerate behavioral slips or relapses in managing her problem behaviors

By supplying basic education related to the dieting or purging exceptions unique to the client; by scaling, normalizing, and reframing; and by determining the circle of influence, the therapist continues to guide therapeutic conversations in a manner that helps the client gain an increased awareness of her internal resources and personal competencies.

When the client does not report changes or continues to talk about the problem (not solutions), my colleagues and I find the failure rests with our inability to negotiate a mutually agreed-upon goal as the central focus of treatment. If the client is not reporting any changes by the third session, we share our concern with the client, taking full responsibility, and then we refocus by asking her: "What do you want to see different as a result of your being here?" This usually gets treatment back on track, unless the client defines a goal that the therapist is unwilling to work on. Goal formulation must be a *mutual* process. However, as therapists, we do have some say in whether or not we are willing to work with the client on her designated goal.

For example, one woman seeking treatment for her eating disorder turned out to be specifically seeking a letter from me verifying that she was in therapy so she could participate in a fasting program. I told her I was not willing to do that, given my opposition to fasting programs. In addition, I also gave her specific information related to the adverse physiological consequences of fasting and restricting, at which time we terminated treatment.

In another case, a client identified a need to have a significant relationship with me as her therapist. After three sessions of trying to deconstruct this goal into something that was transferable into her life, we had this exchange:

THERAPIST: [Mary], it seems to me that you are looking to come here and simply talk about your past so that you can feel connected to someone, is that right?

CLIENT: Yeah. That's what I need. I told you that I just recently terminated a significant relationship, and I just need to have someone to talk with.

THERAPIST: Well, I need to tell you that, although I agree with you that you need someone to talk with at this time, I cannot be that person. You see, Mary, I am not a part of your life. Therapy is not a normal relationship. It is one in which the therapist and client agree to work on a specific goal so that the client's life can be better.

CLIENT: But there aren't any people out there like you. I mean I need someone like you to talk to.

THERAPIST: Well, I'm afraid that is not possible. Now, if you wish to work on how you can find someone in your life that you could talk to, I could agree to that.

Mary was reluctant to work on that goal so therapy terminated, with the door being left open if she should change her mind.

This chapter has presented the skills needed to conduct the first and second sessions. The next chapter is devoted to presenting the solution-based tools and strategies that will take the therapist beyond the second session and help her or him deal with more challenging cases.

Six

Working with Challenging Cases: Useful Interventions

"Would you tell me, please, which way I ought to go
from here?"
   "That depends a good deal on where you want
to get to," said the Cat.
   "I don't much care where— . . . so long as I get
somewhere," Alice added as an explanation.
   "Oh, you're sure to do that," said the Cat, "if you
only walk long enough."

—*Lewis Carroll*
Alice's Adventures in Wonderland

When a client requires more than the first and second session tactics outlined in the last chapter, I have discovered that the following techniques and strategies promote therapeutic conversations about solutions, resiliencies, and client competencies and are particularly useful tools in treating more challenging cases.

Circle of Influence

This technique, a variation of the scaling described in Chapter Five, can be used with visually oriented clients. The client is given an 8½- by 11-inch blank sheet of paper and is asked to imagine that the paper represents her current life. She is then instructed to draw a circle that represents her problem eating behaviors. Next she is to write out, anywhere in the circle, her specific complaints regarding binging, purging, or restricting. Finally, she is asked to draw another circle within the original circle. The second circle is to represent the level of influence or control she believes she has over her problem behaviors. When the client is done, she and the therapist discuss the size of the circle of influence or control, focusing on the following questions and issues. (In this discussion, the therapist must encourage the client to be as specific as possible in identifying behaviors that have contributed to the size of the circle of influence, no matter how small it is.)

- How did your circle of influence get to be that size?
- What do you have to do to maintain your current level of influence or control?
- What has to happen to increase the size of the circle of influence or control by one-half inch?
- Knowing yourself as well as you do, indicate realistically where your circle of influence will be when you are finished with treatment.

The circle of influence assignment can be used throughout the course of treatment and is particularly helpful in maintaining treatment focus. This visual tool not only helps both client and therapist stay on track but also can be generalized to concerns other than eating disorders. When such additional problems are presented, the therapist can encourage the client to use the circle of influence strategy so that she can begin addressing these problems on her own.

Continuing to Explore Exceptions

As mentioned in Chapter One, I strongly believe that the issue of self-efficacy and the role it plays in the eating disorders is a pivotal factor in the treatment process. For many bulimics, self-efficacy has been deeply impaired. Their many attempts to control their behavior have only served to reinforce their own perceived inadequacies. This negative feedback loop, in conjunction with the physiological ramifications of dieting, perpetuates an abysmal sense of helplessness and despair. And this pervasive sense of ineffectiveness keeps them trapped in the binge/purge cycle. An individual's percepts of self-efficacy are a steppingstone in determining the quality of her self-esteem and serve to mediate behavior (DiClemente, Prochaska, & Gibertini, 1985). When an individual perceives herself as efficacious in tasks or situations that are highly valued by her, she will generally feel a sense of competence and thus experience a more positive level of self-esteem. Since the eating disorder client's perception of self-efficacy is greatly diminished, the focus of treatment should attempt to modify the client's percepts related to her levels of self-efficacy particularly in the areas of her dietary practices and purging activities. By focusing on the client's own mastery experiences related to eating, restricting, and purging behaviors, further entrenchment in the maladaptive behaviors is thwarted or reduced and the individual is likely to experience a positive ripple effect that influences other aspects of her life.

According to Bandura (1982a), an individual's judgments of self-efficacy, whether accurate or fallacious, are based on four principal sources of information, three of which are germane to our discussion:

1. Enactive or performance attainments, which provide the most influential source of efficacy data because they are founded on authentic mastery experiences. Success increases percepts of self-efficacy, while repeated failures decrease them.

2. Vicarious experiences, in which the individual observes similar others performing successfully and, thus, heightening their percepts of self-efficacy. In addition to social comparison, competent models also can teach observers useful strategies for dealing with difficult or problematic situations.

3. Verbal persuasion, in which the individual is persuaded to believe that she has the resources needed to achieve her goals. Persuasive efficacy influences have the greatest leverage on those individuals who believe their actions can create change.

According to Bandura (1982a), these modes of influence are significant in terms of cognitive appraisal. The cognitive processing of efficacy information is based on the types of cues people have acquired as a measure of their personal efficacy. "If self-efficacy is lacking, people tend to behave ineffectually, even though they know what to do. Social learning theory postulates a common mechanism of behavioral change—different modes of influence alter coping behavior partly by creating and strengthening self-percepts of efficacy" (Bandura, 1982a, p. 127).

In integrating self-efficacy theory with solution-focused therapy, the following techniques specifically serve to promote self-efficacy:

1. Exceptions promote self-efficacy through highlighting, amplifying and reinforcing enactive mastery skills.

2. Exceptions in group therapy promote self-efficacy through vicarious modes of influence.

3. Therapeutic compliments serve to function as a means of persuasive influence in increasing self-efficacy.

Enactive or Performance Attainments

By exploring those times when the client is doing something different from the problem behavior, the therapist reveals that the client has had mastery experiences, thus strengthening the client's perceptions of self-efficacy. Initially, the therapeutic conversation heightens the client's awareness of her current mastery experiences. In the following sample conversation, I am talking with a returning client who has been away at college.

THERAPIST: So what's better since I saw you last?

CLIENT [*smiling*]: Well, I maintained my weight!

THERAPIST: No kidding! That's great. How have you been doing that?

CLIENT: Well, remember how we talked about how much better I was last school year? When I was carefree and going out with my friends and my anorexia wasn't so bad?

THERAPIST: Yeah. I remember.

CLIENT: Well, I remembered that one of the things I used to do then was to go out for lunch with my sister, "Carrie." It's strange you know. When we'd go out, even though it was still hard for me to eat, somehow, it was just a little bit easier. I mean like I would eat a couple of french fries and even have a little bit of her milk shake.

THERAPIST: Really?

CLIENT: Yeah. So that's what I have been doing! Since she is on campus too, I have been asking her to have lunch with me on a weekly basis. That has really made a difference for me. I don't seem to be restricting as much at the other lunch times.

THERAPIST: Wow. That's really terrific. I know that took a lot of hard work.

CLIENT: It sure did. It really is hard, you know.

THERAPIST: I'm sure it is. How were you able to do this? I'm impressed.

CLIENT: Well, I don't know. I mean, I just know I don't want to have to go back in the hospital, and Carrie really worries about me.

THERAPIST: You really love your sister a lot. It seems as though that's what helps you stay out of the hospital.

CLIENT: Yeah. You're right. When I think of her and how she worried about me last time . . . I just don't want to go back in the hospital.

THERAPIST: So this love you have for Carrie is what really helps you right now?

CLIENT: Yup.

Highlighting what was different for this client and a continued focus on what helped her maintain her weight served to increase her perceptions of self-efficacy related to her restrictive eating behaviors.

Some common questions that are useful in focusing on exceptions are:

- Are there times when your binging/purging doesn't occur?
- What's different about those times? (Be sure to get specific details, such as, who, what, where, and when.)
- Can you think of any other times when your binging or purging is less of a problem? Even just a little bit less?
- How was it that you were able to eat that cracker? I know how very difficult that must have been for you. How did you do that?
- What helps you the most to resist the urge to binge or purge? Exercise?
- What helps you the most to resist the urge not to eat?
- Tell me how you stopped binging? Purging? How did that happen? How come you didn't keep right on binging or purging? How come it didn't get worse?
- How come you didn't start binging or purging as soon as you got up the next day? (If client reports evening or daytime binges only.)
- Tell me how your binging/purging/restricting is different than it was when you sought counseling for the very first time? Before you were hospitalized?
- How does your day go differently when you are not binging/purging/restricting?
- What do you suppose will have to happen so you can continue to be in control of your binging/purging?
- What surprised you most about yourself and your eating since I last saw you?

Other exception-related questions that are helpful are relational in nature (Miller, 1992b). Since much of the client's self-view is influenced by others' perceptions, the therapist focuses on what significant others would perceive as different about the client during those exceptional times.

- If I were to ask your spouse (parent or employer) what he (she) noticed is different about you on those days you're not restricting/binging/purging, what do you suppose he (she) might say?

- Who else might notice what's different about you on those days you are not binging/purging/restricting?

- How could you tell that he (she) noticed?

- What might he (she) say has to happen for you to stop binging/purging/restricting more frequently?

- When you are not binging/purging/restricting, what do you notice is different about your spouse (parents or employer)?

- What might he (she) say is different about himself (herself) when you are not binging/purging/restricting?

- If I were to ask your spouse (parent or friend) what has surprised them the most about you since you started treatment, what might they say?

Vicarious Modes of Influence

Just as exploring for exceptions in individual therapy can highlight the client's enactive mastery experiences, highlighting group members' exceptions in group therapy can promote vicarious mastery experiences through both social comparison and modeling.

As will be discussed in much greater detail in Chapter Seven, solution-focused group therapy directs group norms toward highlighting and reinforcing exceptions much like individual therapy does, so that group members are sharing solution patterns rather than focusing on problems and dysfunctions. Participating in an ongoing group allows for all three types of self-efficacy modes. However, group therapy is a more direct approach in achieving vicariously learned self-efficacy experiences.

Persuasive Modes of Influence

Verbal persuasion is another mode of influence that is used to get people to believe they possess capabilities that will enable them to achieve their goals (Bandura, 1982a). Persuasive efficacy influences have the greatest impact on those individuals who believe they can create change through their own actions. Thus, persuasive influences are most effective within a customer-type relationship.

The persuasive influence that is most commonly used in the solution-focused model is the therapeutic compliment. According to deShazer (1988), the purpose of the compliments is to build a "yes set" that helps to get the client into a frame of mind to accept something new, that is, the therapeutic task or directive.

Erickson's concept of the "yes set" forms the cornerstone for the notion of the compliment as promoting client cooperation (Erickson & Rossi, 1981). In this technique, the therapist delivers a series of statements to which the client would agree. These statements are followed by a suggestion that the client is led to agree with as a result of it being linked to the series.

Although the solution-focused model uses compliments as a means of "selling" the intervention to the client, therapeutic compliments can serve other purposes as well, particularly in increasing client's percepts of self-efficacy. *Webster's Dictionary* defines *compliment* as (1) an expression of esteem, respect, affection or admiration or (2) formal and respectful recognition.

Because many clients discount or minimize their own efforts in managing their eating behaviors, therapeutic compliments are a way for the therapist to formally recognize the client's successes and hard work in achieving her goals, thus influencing her perceptions of her own capabilities. Here are two examples of persuasive compliments that work in this way.

> THERAPIST: I am really impressed with your determination to stop purging. The steps you have taken—removing all binge foods from your house, going for a walk or calling a friend immediately after you have eaten dinner, and maintaining a journal of your successes—are an indication that you are making significant progress. Based on my clinical experience with similar individuals, you are doing exceedingly well. You are to be congratulated for your hard work.
>
> THERAPIST: Given that you have been able to maintain abstinence in the past for lengthy periods and based on my clinical experience, I am confident that you will be able to achieve this abstinence again, provided you are willing to work at it as you were then.

Therapeutic compliments must be delivered sincerely by the therapist and paced according to the client's reactions to them. Although persuasive compliments are most useful in a customer-type relationship or when the client is in the action stage of change, therapeutic compliments within visitor- and complainant-type relationships also have benefit in that they can serve to strengthen the therapeutic alliance and pave the way for increased cooperation. These compliments need to be less persuasive in content and more general to the positive changes the client is making. For example,

> THERAPIST: Even though it wasn't your idea to come here today, I feel as though I must compliment you for respecting your parents' wishes. Based on what you have told me and the fact that you're here, I believe that you must love them very much.

THERAPIST: I know that you are feeling quite frustrated since you have had several "slips" in being able to "control" your eating. However, I feel as though I must compliment you on your tenacity. You really have this "strong desire" to keep on working at it. The fact that you continue to come here is just one indication that you really are a "fighter" (client's language in quotes).

Since eating disorder clients tend toward perfectionism, they have a tendency to discount or minimize the changes they make as being significant. The use of compliments or feedback is helpful at this point in reinforcing the changes.

THERAPIST: From what I hear you saying, I gather these steps don't seem that significant to you. But, I must emphasize that based on my clinical experience with similar individuals, you are doing exactly what you need to be doing in order to reach your goal.

Rather than trying to convince the client that her changes are significant or noteworthy, sometimes it is helpful to express confusion regarding her discounting or minimizing them.

THERAPIST: I must compliment you on the changes you have made since our last session. However, from what I hear you saying, they don't seem to mean that much to you. I am somewhat confused by this. Can you tell me what might be a more significant sign to you that you are making progress?

Regardless of the type of compliment delivered, a review of our tapes indicates that clients are genuinely appreciative of the compliment and often express surprise at achievements highlighted by the therapist.

Scaling

In the last chapter, I touched on scaling as it is used in the first session. However, scales are extremely versatile and limited only by
the therapist's imagination. Scales can be used to measure such
things as self-confidence, self-esteem, self-efficacy in tasks related
to eating behaviors, and willingness to change. They are extremely
useful in keeping the client and therapist focused on treatment
progress. For example, in working with an anorexic who began for
the first time to experience feelings of rage toward her grandfather
who grossly sexually abused her, I used a scale to help her develop
a comfort level with feelings that she had described as terribly
frightening, both in the session and the day before when she had
called to tell me just how frightened she was of her rage.

CLIENT: I am really afraid that if I let myself feel this rage I will
lose it. I mean really lose it.

THERAPIST: So on a scale of 0 to 10, with 10 being "losing it"
and 0 being the farthest thing from it, where were you
yesterday when you called me.

CLIENT: Let's see. I was probably at a 5.

THERAPIST: So tell me then, what was helpful in managing
these angry feelings when you were as high as a 5 yesterday?

CLIENT: Well, at first I stomped around the house. I was really
pissed off.

THERAPIST: What else was helpful when you were at a 5 on the
scale?

CLIENT: After a while, I distracted myself and went out and
bought my husband a birthday gift. That helped. But only
for a while.

THERAPIST: So then what else helped you manage your anger?

CLIENT: Then I called you and that helped. And then when my
husband came home, I talked some more to him, I mean like
we talked for hours. He really listened to me.

The client and I continued to use this scale to help her develop a measure of her ability to tolerate her feelings, along with specific coping strategies.

When it is focused on the gains made from previous therapy, scaling can also solidify changes.

THERAPIST: So you've had two years of individual therapy.

CLIENT: Yup. Probably about one and a half on a weekly basis, and then I just couldn't face the issues I really needed to work on.

THERAPIST: Maybe it was just time to take a break. You strike me as someone who would work really hard in therapy.

CLIENT: Yeah, I guess I really did work hard. I never thought about it as needing a break. I thought I just couldn't face the sex abuse.

THERAPIST: Maybe it wasn't the right time.

CLIENT: Yeah, maybe it wasn't. But I'm ready now.

THERAPIST: Great. Let me ask you this. On a scale from 0 to 10, 10 being where you want to be when you're finished with therapy and 0 being where you were when you walked into your last therapist's office, where are you today on that scale?

CLIENT: Hm . . . interesting question. I'd say about a 6.

THERAPIST: A 6. You really did do a lot of work last time. Tell me how you were able to get as high as a 6.

The client and I then spent the entire session reviewing the specific changes she had made as a result of her last counseling experience, and afterward, she spontaneously commented, "Maybe I'm not as bad off as I thought!"

Scaling is particularly effective with anorexics. In the following conversation from my second session with a fourteen-year-old anorexic who identified her goal for treatment as wanting to stay out of the hospital and stop having to see doctors, the client and I negotiated a scale that we then used throughout therapy.

THERAPIST: So if 10 represents your anorexia at its worst, when you were in the hospital last summer, and 0 is its complete absence, that is you are "rid of it," where do you fall today?

CLIENT: Oh, probably an 8.

THERAPIST: So, tell me, how you have been able to go from a 10 to an 8?

CLIENT: Well, I guess I admitted that I had it.

THERAPIST: That's really different for you, to admit it. What else?

CLIENT: I just wanted to get rid of those people in the hospital, and I knew what I had to do. I just don't want to be in the hospital again.

THERAPIST: So what did you have to do to go from a 10 to an 8?

CLIENT: I'd eat more.

THERAPIST: When you were at a 10, how was your eating then?

CLIENT: I guess I'd eat a piece of lettuce . . . that was a lot.

THERAPIST: So, how is it different today, when you're at an 8?

CLIENT: Well, I'll eat different stuff. Like one cup of dry cereal in the morning. I'll even let myself chew one stick of gum a week. But that's about it.

THERAPIST: What's the lowest you ever got on that scale?

CLIENT: Oh, probably about a 3.

THERAPIST: Now when was that?

CLIENT: Right after Christmas.

THERAPIST: So tell me what's better when you're at a 3 on the scale?

CLIENT: Well, I wasn't going to doctors.

THERAPIST: So everyone was off your back?

CLIENT: Yeah. I guess I wasn't so worried then, and I wasn't thinking about it all of the time. It comes before everything—my plans with friends. I say no; I can't go out because . . . well, I just think about it all the time.

THERAPIST: So when you were at a 3 on the scale, how were things different?

CLIENT: I would go out more and be more carefree.

THERAPIST: And so how are you different when you are more carefree?

The therapist and client can continue to explore this kind of exception in greater detail and then move into a discussion related to the formulation of a specific goal. In this case, the client had depicted herself as being "carefree" on her miracle day, and this idea continued to emerge throughout therapy as the quality she wanted to see in her life.

Scaling questions can also help the client develop cues for changing the course of a binge or a purge, as illustrated in the next conversation.

THERAPIST: On a scale from 0 to 10, with 0 being the actual binge or purge and 10 being you are in control, where on the scale are you *first* aware that you are beginning to lose control?

CLIENT: Oh, about a 4.

THERAPIST: That's great. Lot's of people I work with have to start at 0! Now, how can you tell you're at a 4?

CLIENT: Well, I start obsessing about food and whether or not I have what I want to eat in the house. It's like a hum in my head.

THERAPIST: What would you need to do differently the next time you are at a 4?

CLIENT: I'd have to probably refocus, you know, think about something else.

THERAPIST: Like what?

CLIENT: Like how lousy I'm gonna feel if I actually binge.

THERAPIST: How would that be helpful?

CLIENT: Well, I know I end up feeling bloated, and my throat hurts like hell. I hate that feeling.

THERAPIST: So the next time you're at a 4, you'd do what?

CLIENT: Well, I'd refocus and think about how much better I'll feel about myself not only mentally but physically.

THERAPIST: When most recently have you felt like that?

CLIENT: I guess it was this morning when I didn't binge. I felt really good about myself and more energetic.

THERAPIST: So this morning is kind of like an anchor point that you can use when you're at a 4 on the scale again?

CLIENT: Yeah.

THERAPIST: What other recent anchor points can you hang on to when you're at a 4 on the scale?

CLIENT: Well, last weekend when I was visiting my sister, same thing happened. I didn't binge, and I felt great about myself, you know, happier and more energetic.

THERAPIST: Okay. Now, what would you have to do to increase your control by one level. That is, go from a 4 to a 5?

CLIENT: Gee, I don't know. [*Pauses.*] Well, after I'd refocus, I guess it would help to actually do something. You know, to keep me occupied.

THERAPIST: So what did you do this morning?

CLIENT: Let's see. I left the house early so I could get myself some coffee and a muffin at the bakery. Getting out of the house really helped.

THERAPIST: And what did you do last weekend at your sister's?

CLIENT: Let's see. I was more active. In the morning, she and I went out for a walk. It was a great day.

THERAPIST: So when you are at a 4, you will refocus and think about how much better you will feel, using this morning as an anchor point and maybe even the morning you were at your sister's?

CLIENT: Yeah.

THERAPIST: And what will you do to increase your control by one level. That is go from a 4 to a 5?

CLIENT: I'll do something outside the house.

Through this kind of conversation about scales, the client establishes a measure for self-efficacy in moving toward negotiated goals.

When clients express unrealistic goals or wish to make gigantic leaps in managing their problematic behaviors, it is very helpful to use scales.

CLIENT: What I really want to be able to do is . . . to tell my mother off. You know, she really pisses me off. I know that if I could just tell her what I *really* think, I would absolutely stop binging and purging. I just know it.

THERAPIST: So, *knowing yourself as well as you do* [*said slowly and deliberately*], how likely is it that you could really tell your mother that she pisses you off?

CLIENT [*laughs*]: Well, it's a great fantasy. But it's probably not very likely. I mean, I'm just not that kind of person.

THERAPIST: So let's say that on a scale of 0 to 10, with 10 being you could really tell your mother how much she pisses you off and 0 being the farthest thing from it, *knowing yourself as well as you do* [*again said slowly and deliberately*], what's the absolute highest you could go on that scale?

CLIENT: Oh, gee, probably a 7.

THERAPIST: Okay. So describe to me what you will be doing when you are at a 7.

In such situations, the client and therapist pursue this line of thought until the specific details that describe the general goal in concrete and behavioral terms are clearly established. Then the therapist seeks to discover where the client is on the scale today. This begins the process of establishing the client's current level of functioning, which can then be followed by a delineation of subgoals, that is, what would have to happen in order for her to move up one level on the scale.

During the interview just cited, the client and I explored exceptions to identify those times she was able to express her feelings of anger toward her mother. Then these exceptions were integrated into the solution pattern.

Challenging Negative Mindsets

Paying attention to client language laden with such words as "never," "always," "should," "can't," "must," "have to," "could have," or "if only" can give the therapist a way to challenge the client's cognitive distortions. When the client uses one of these negative generalizations, the therapist needs to question the client directly regarding her statement.

CLIENT: I have never been able to eat normally. I can remember when I was a kid and my mom would—

THERAPIST: Wait a minute. Where do you get that idea . . . that you have never been able to eat normally?

CLIENT: Uh, well, it's true. I just don't have normal eating habits.

THERAPIST: So where did you get that idea?

CLIENT: Uh, well, I don't know. I just don't think I do.

THERAPIST: So what's normal?

CLIENT: I guess three meals a day.

THERAPIST: So where did you get that idea?

CLIENT [*laughing*]: I don't know! I guess from my mom and from what I've read.

THERAPIST: Hm. I don't eat three meals a day. Actually, I know lots of people who don't eat three meals a day.

CLIENT: Well, maybe normal isn't three meals a day, but it doesn't matter. I have abnormal eating habits.

THERAPIST: Well, let's take a look at what's normal and then maybe you can make a better decision about whether or not your eating is abnormal.

At the conclusion of this discussion, the client expressed great confusion about whether her eating was in fact abnormal. She and

I spent the remainder of the session focused on what *was* normal for her, based on an exploration of her exceptions. In this particular case, the client identified that she was never hungry in the morning and did not eat breakfast. However, at midmorning she would have a candy bar or pastry because she was really hungry then. Then her guilt would be so intense that she wouldn't eat at lunchtime but would end up binging at around two or three o'clock in the afternoon.

In defining what was normal for her, she and I negotiated her mealtimes so that they related to her internal clock. Her breakfast was designated to take place at 10:00 A.M. and lunch at 2:30 P.M. An exploration of exceptions also revealed that when she brought snacks and lunch to work she was much less likely to go to the vending machines supplied with high-fat snack foods.

Seeding doubts in a client about the negative labels she uses can be equally powerful in getting her to reevaluate her mindsets.

THERAPIST: Tell me what brings you in for counseling?

CLIENT: Well, I have this eating disorder. I'm bulimic.

THERAPIST: I'm curious. How did you come to this conclusion . . . that you have an eating disorder.

CLIENT: Well, I binge and purge. I guess that means I have an eating disorder.

THERAPIST: Well, you know, research demonstrates that lots of so-called normal women engage in binging and/or purging behaviors to mitigate weight gain. That doesn't necessarily mean they are bulimic.

CLIENT: Huh. I just thought I was.

THERAPIST: Well, maybe you're not. Tell me more, from your viewpoint, about the more normal aspects of your relationship with food.

In this case, I tried to plant seeds of doubt about the veracity of the client's view of herself as bulimic by first exploring her view of what was normal about her eating.

Other negative mindsets in which eating disorder clients tend to become entangled include, but certainly are not limited to, the following. The client

- Believes that her basic worth is measured by the kind of foods she consumes. For example, she deems herself "good" when she consumes healthy low-fat food and "bad" when she consumes high-calorie, high-fat food.
- Believes that a thin body will guarantee her a perfect life of eternal happiness.
- Believes that she should always be happy and never experience negative feelings.
- Believes that the ideal is real and achievable.

In challenging these mindsets, the most effective tools the therapist can utilize are humor, normalizing, reframing, and simple direct challenges.

Pattern Intervention

Many eating disorder clients have established patterns related to their binging, purging, or restricting behaviors. Therefore, helping the client recognize her unique pattern can be a useful tool in altering the behavior.

In our experience at EDRC, identifying the pattern is a crucial early step in treatment. Some clients have only a limited and often skewed awareness of the details of their eating, purging, or restricting behaviors, and this limitation makes it difficult for client and therapist to negotiate a meaningful homework task. This difficulty is particularly common among clients who have had no previous treatment or did not reach the action stage of change in their former treatment experience.

Pattern intervention rests upon the assumption that change is generative; thus, the therapist must focus on the ripple effects of the altered pattern and what becomes different as a result.

Two strategies facilitate the identification of the client's idiosyncratic patterns. The first is especially effective with clients in a complainant relationship and at the contemplation stage of change. In this strategy, the therapist simultaneously probes for exceptions and pays close attention to the emerging patterns of the problem behaviors as described by the client. This information is then highlighted by the therapist, helping the client see the specifics of who, what, where, when, and why, so that the client has the opportunity not only to see the pattern but also to consider possible ways of altering it. The following brief case studies illustrate both the usefulness of this strategy and its ripple effect.

Case Study

"Barb" sought counseling because she was purging five to eight times a day. This adolescent was chewing her nails every night so that it would be easier to use her index finger to induce vomiting. After an extensive discussion of her binge-purge patterns, and having other information supplied by the client that revealed she was terribly ashamed of her hands because her fingers looked so ugly and stubby, I asked her to toss a coin every evening to determine if she would simply not chew her nails on those evenings the coin came up heads and instead would paint her nails. If she wanted to purge the next day, she first had to remove the nail polish.

Barb returned three weeks later, proudly showing off her longer, painted nails, and casually mentioned that she had not purged since her last session. The remainder of the session focused on what was different, how she maintained her nails and what helped her to not bite, and how this affected her purging. I ended the session by using a self-confidence scale, on which the client gave herself a 7.

Case Study

"Megan," a forty-seven-year-old anorexic, had recently begun purging after eating. After we discussed her patterns in detail, what clearly emerged was that she *never* purged when she was eating out and was with other people. I directed her to toss a coin the next three times she was eating with other people. When the coin turned up heads, she was to force herself to purge and notice what was different.

Paradox Task

One month later, Megan returned and reported that her purging at home had decreased significantly. As we identified what was different and what was helping her control her urge to purge, she digressed and told me that she had tried the task and that, although she tried to purge when she was with other people, she just could not make herself do it. She reported that she was so struck by the fact that she could not make herself purge, she decided that she was going to try to make herself stop purging at home.

Pattern intervention can be an especially powerful intervention with eating disorder clients; however, the rapport that exists between the client and therapist is a critical factor in the success of these therapeutic directives. The importance of a relationship based on collaboration and mutuality can never be underestimated in the implementation of any of the strategies discussed here. In addition, as Cade and O'Hanlon (1993) point out, the therapist should ask herself or himself, "Is the intervention targeting some aspect of the client's or family's life in which they are emotionally invested and also in which they have an investment that a solution be found? If this is not the case, clients will be unlikely to follow the suggestions and thus, patterns will remain unchanged" (p. 134).

A second pattern intervention, which is most effective within a customer relationship and at the action stage of change, uses food records that allow the client, therapist, and nutritionist to assess client eating patterns as well as nutritional deficiencies and strengths. A food record should be arranged so that it helps the client document the following information for a designated period of time: food intake; time and place of eating and whom the client ate with; mood; hunger level (on a 0 to 5 scale for example); purging activities; type, frequency, and duration of exercise activities; consumption of basic food groups; and observations and reflections.

Once a food record is completed and returned, the therapist and client discuss what the client noticed as she filled out the food record. Many clients report a heightened awareness of their patterns from keeping the record and, as a result, have already spontaneously initiated changes in their eating and purging. Therefore, the therapist must help the client see such exceptions more clearly and must reinforce any changes that have occurred as a result of the task, using such questions as

- How did you get that to happen?
- How was your day better?
- What did others notice that was different about you on your better days?
- What did you notice that was different about yourself?
- How can you continue to make this happen?

Since a food record seems on the surface to focus on the problem behavior, it is not uncommon for therapists discussing these records to be sidetracked into debating why the client engages in particular eating behaviors. Therefore, the therapist must work to maintain a focus on the changes the client experienced and avoid segueing into talk of the problem.

Food records serve a dual purpose when they are also used by a nutritionist and the client to assess nutritional deficiencies and strengths in relation to the client's weight and physical condition. The nutritionist, too, must focus on what the client is already doing that is nutritionally sound rather than on the poor behavior and then negotiate a client-based food plan (see Chapter Seven).

Comparison Pictures and Basic Education

The most powerful interventions employ the techniques the client already uses in managing her eating, purging, or restricting behaviors. In order to get clients to view these existing techniques as meaningful and to realize that their ideal goal of never having the desire to binge, purge, or restrict is unrealistic in the short-run, the therapist must deconstruct this ideal global goal to a more achievable goal. In this deconstruction, it is useful for the therapist to provide both a comparison picture and basic education about the physiological properties of dieting and purging.

To create a comparison picture, the therapist gives direct feedback to the client about her exceptions and solution patterns as they compare to those of similar clients. This picture, as illustrated in the following therapeutic conversation, can reinforce what the client is doing and encourage her to develop more realistic expectations of herself and set more attainable goals.

THERAPIST: So you haven't binged or purged for the last week?

CLIENT: Yeah, but I did this morning. So what difference does it make? I did it this morning; I wasn't able to focus like I did last week.

THERAPIST: You know, I have to tell you that, based on my clinical experience with young women similar to you, what you did this past week is no small feat. Actually, it's pretty incredible. Many clients with a similar history aren't able to do what you did. They generally aren't ready to actually do something different at this point in therapy. You figured out that this whole thing takes hard work and that by focusing in the morning and writing down your commitment to abstinence and planning your meals you were able to continue maintaining your goal. I feel as though I must compliment you.

CLIENT: You mean other people you've worked with don't do as well?

THERAPIST: Absolutely. A week of abstinence is a very good sign. Tell me again how you were able to do this.

Basic education about the physiological effects of her behavior shows the client that more is involved in changing that behavior than just will power. Since her behavior has altered her metabolism and brain chemistry, relapse is to be expected, and changing her pattern will take a great deal of hard work. This information neutralizes the self-blame many of these clients feel when they are, in their view, too weak to eradicate (or control) the behavior. In addition, such education promotes self-efficacy, since the therapist reinforces the client's mastery experiences with the behavior while diffusing the client's personalization of the behavior.

My conversation with the client whom I complimented for not binging for a week, continued with just such education. I said to her, "Somehow, you have this notion that this binging and purging is simply a matter of will power. Although I agree with you, there is another piece to the puzzle. A very important piece. Given the length of time you have been binging and purging, you have altered your metabolism; thus, it is expected that you might relapse. Let me give you this fact sheet so you really know what you are up against. We can then take a look at what you might have done differently this morning to prevent this relapse."

Inner Dialogue

A review of EDRC therapy session tapes shows that a vast majority of eating disorder clients report that self-talk messages, or inner dialogues, are a critical factor in altering their problem behaviors for the better. Clients often are unclear about the specific thoughts or events that helped them when they experienced exceptions to their behaviors, and it may be helpful for the therapist to direct

clients to an increased awareness of inner dialogues. This process
of direction may require a great deal of patience on the part of the
therapist before the client can identify in detail the specific self-talk
messages she has used.

THERAPIST: So what do you suppose was different yesterday
afternoon, when you didn't purge even after you had eaten
all that cake?

CLIENT: I don't know. It was really weird. Here I had had three
pieces of cake, and I just decided I wasn't going to throw it
up. It was really hard, I can't tell you how hard it was.

THERAPIST: So what helped you the most? I mean, this is a
really difficult thing to do . . . not to purge.

CLIENT: I just decided. I bet it won't last.

THERAPIST: Well, let's walk through the episode. You ate the
cake, right? Here you were, feeling uncomfortably full,
like you had many times before . . . so, how did you stop
yourself?

CLIENT: Well, I just told myself that I would only feel worse if I
threw up.

THERAPIST: So you talked to yourself? That's what helped you
through? Telling yourself you would only feel worse? What
else did you tell yourself?

CLIENT: Well, I thought about how my throat would hurt and
how my stomach would be bloated. So, I said to myself that
I wasn't going to throw up, no matter what. I am sick and
tired of feeling like shit. [Laughing.] You know, this other
voice said, "You feel like shit now. If you just throw up, you'll
feel better. Go ahead and do it."

THERAPIST: So how come you didn't listen to that voice?

CLIENT: I don't know. The other voice told it to shut up.
[Laughs.]

THERAPIST: So you had this conversation with yourself and
by thinking about the consequences of your purging and

telling yourself that you weren't going to throw up, you were able to stop? Wow! That's terrific! What did you do then?

CLIENT: I walked out of the kitchen, talking to myself all of the way, got into my car, and drove around for a while until I felt safe.

THERAPIST: So when you felt safe, what were you saying to yourself then?

CLIENT: . . . I guess I was telling myself how proud I was that I stopped myself. It felt really good to know that I could stop myself.

THERAPIST: Tell me again, what helped you the most to stop yourself?

Accessing such inner dialogue is valuable precisely because it is the dialogue that the client has developed as a means of controlling her problem behaviors. By highlighting and amplifying this dialogue, the therapist helps the client increase her awareness of this self-formulated tool that has proven useful in achieving her goal. Once again, a mastery experience is identified, and the client feels a greater sense of self-efficacy. Here is another example of a conversation about these important inner dialogues.

THERAPIST: So tell me again, you have this urge to eat but you didn't. Walk me through what you did differently.

CLIENT: The first step was, "No, I can't do this any more." I knew that I would eat as long as I just sat there in my apartment.

THERAPIST: The second step?

CLIENT: I said to myself, "I need to get out of here." So I physically took myself somewhere else. I went to Barnes & Noble, that huge bookstore. I love books, you know. I can get lost in that place.

THERAPIST: Now, that was different for you?

CLIENT: I do that a lot. But it was different in that I could actually concentrate on the stuff I was reading.

THERAPIST: So how do you account for that difference?

CLIENT: Well, I acknowledged the fact that I couldn't get my mind off food. It's really stupid. I mean someone says, "Don't think about pink elephants." So what do you do? So I said to myself, "Okay, I'm going to think about food. It's okay if I think about food."

THERAPIST: That really helped?

CLIENT: You bet. You know, the first place I went to in the bookstore was the cookbook section! I said to myself, "Let's get this out of your system." So I looked at pictures of chocolate for few minutes, and you know what? I haven't been able to eat chocolate for the past five days!

Further along in this interview, I emphasized the client's inner dialogue by repeating it back to her, and I amplified the changes she was able to make between sessions. This client was able to expand her inner dialogue and use it consistently to help manage her binge behaviors.

Another client, an adolescent anorexic, referenced what she called her anorexic voice and her healthy voice.

THERAPIST: So what's better since our last session?

CLIENT: Well, you'll never believe this.

THERAPIST: So give me a try.

CLIENT: You know how we all went to that [university] open house . . . for prospective students last weekend?

THERAPIST: Yeah. I remember. Your whole family went to see the campus. How did your sister like it?

CLIENT: She loves it and has decided to go there.

THERAPIST: That's great. So tell me what I'll never believe.

CLIENT: Well, we all went to a restaurant, and I actually ordered something from the menu and ate it in front of my parents! Can you believe that?

THERAPIST: That's terrific! How did you do that?

CLIENT: Well, it seems as though my healthy voice is getting louder than my anorexic voice. That healthy voice said, "Go ahead and order that vegetable plate. It will be okay. If you eat that now, you won't have to skip a meal and then your weight won't drop and then you won't have to keep going to Dr. [Smith] for those dumb weigh-ins."

THERAPIST: I'm sure your anorexic voice wasn't mute.

CLIENT: Of course not. But the healthy voice just told it to shut up. [*Laughs.*]

THERAPIST: So what has to happen so that healthy voice can get even louder?

The client and I began to explore what she would have to do first to help her healthy voice maintain itself, and then we discussed what she would have to do in order to "get it louder." She decided that the healthy voice needed to give her more affirming messages, which specifically included such self-talk as "Take it nice and easy" and "Being healthy is much more fun than being sick."

Before-and-After Task

The before-and-after task accesses client resources at the same time that it projects the client into the future, to a time in her life when she will have a normal relationship with food. In this task, the client is shown a lifeline marked off in 5-year intervals from 0 to 100 years and is asked to identify exactly when her eating behaviors became problematic. She is to identify what qualities she had, what activities she was involved in, how other people viewed her strengths, and so on, *prior* to the problem. Then she and her therapist talk about what she was like at that time, with the therapist probing for and highlighting strengths and resources.

Next, the client indicates on the lifeline when she believes her relationship with food will normalize. She also identifies the characteristics she will possess at this later point in her life, with an emphasis on how others will view her differently. The therapist then guides the client in an integration of her former and future qualities. She is asked to pay attention to the times when she is already experiencing her future or healed self, and to those times when she feels like her earlier, "normal" self, and to note what is different about those two times.

Many clients are struck by the similarities between their past and future qualities and strengths. Often they are then able to spontaneously identify that the strengths they hope for in the future must already exist and that they are actually using them in their daily lives. This task gives the client hope in the therapeutic process. According to Furman and Ahola (1992), "Since the future is often connected to the past, people with a stressful past are prone to have a hopeless view of their future. In its turn a negative vision of the future exacerbates current problems by casting a pessimistic shadow over both past and present. . . . Fortunately, the converse is also true; a positive view of the future invites hope, and hope in its turn helps to cope with the current hardships, to recognize signs indicating the possibility of change, to view the past as an ordeal rather than a misery, and to provide the inspiration for generating solutions" (p. 91).

Associational Cue for Control and Self-Efficacy

The associational cue for control and self-efficacy is an adaptation of Dolan's associational cue for comfort and safety (1992). Dolan defines an associational cue as a signal that elicits an unconscious response. Once developed, the cue "can provide an alternative to other less healthy ways of dealing with symptoms of pain and anxiety" (p. 101). Thus, in working with eating disorder clients, the therapist helps them identify cues that they can use to control their behavior when they face an urge to purge, binge, or restrict.

Since many eating disorder clients view themselves as weak, inadequate, and lacking in will power and have no way to connect with their inner resources in the midst of a binge-purge or restrictive cycle, an associational cue can give these clients a way to activate a resource.

Therapists can use the following eight steps to help clients develop their own associational cues (adapted from Dolan, 1992, pp. 102–103).

1. Have the client close her eyes and take a few deep breaths. Wait a minute or so as she relaxes, then ask her to think of a recent time when she experienced a sense of personal control and self-efficacy.

2. Ask her to notice and describe the details of this experience, highlighting sights, sounds, and sensations. You can also help the client to expand on her experience.

3. Ask her to simply enjoy the experience for a few minutes in silence.

4. Say to her, "Make any adjustments, additions, or subtractions of details that would further enhance your feelings of personal control and self-efficacy." The client does this quietly. Ask her to nod her head when she is finished.

5. Say to her, "Enjoy the experience one last time . . . and while you are doing this, you are to select a symbol that will remind you of this empowering experience in the future . . . a sort of souvenir." The symbol may be any sight, sound, or sensation that reevokes the experience for the client. Also say to her, "You might like to take a little rest and let your unconscious choose for you, and see what meaningful symbol comes to mind."

6. Ask her to open her eyes and reorient herself to the present. Then ask her to think of the symbol for a moment and notice how it feels to reevoke her state of personal control and self-efficacy.

7. Suggest that she can use this symbol whenever she feels the need to reconnect to a state of personal control and self-efficacy. If she wishes, she can obtain an object that reminds her of this symbol and use that object when appropriate.

8. Instruct her to recall this symbol when she is feeling most out of control and powerless.

The associational cue is a powerful tool that the client can use when she is faced with a binge-purge or other problem episode, or immediately after such an episode, so that she can regain her sense of control and be less likely to continue in the pattern. (This strategy can be taught to groups as well.) In follow-up sessions, clients report that the associational cue is extremely empowering, not only in managing a binge-purge episode but also in other situations in which the client feels out of control.

A variation of this strategy that we use at EDRC is designed to increase the client's cognitive awareness of her idiosyncratic individual cues around her "out-of-control" eating behaviors. By using a scale, clients develop a much clearer awareness and understanding of the specific attitudes and behaviors that serve them as cues when they are

- Building up to a binging, purging, or restricting episode
- Maintaining a state or near-state of calm or control in confronting problem behaviors
- Determining what would be most helpful for them in managing their ability to stay in control

To teach this variant strategy, the therapist asks the client to imagine a scale, with 0 being "in control" of her problem eating behavior and 10 being "out of control." The client then is asked to "describe (or list) what attitudes, thoughts, behaviors, and activities" she experiences at a 0 and at a 10 rating. The therapist's role at this point is to encourage specificity and help the client identify observable behaviors. Once the client has a picture of what a 10 and a 0 mean to her, she is asked to describe what "attitudes, thoughts, behaviors, and activities" she experiences at a 9. (If the client reports that she is always at a 10, the therapist asks her to *imagine* what it would be like at a lower level.) The therapist then has the client continue to identify attitudes, thoughts, and behaviors for each level down to 0, taking ample time to develop the details of each level. Finally, the client is asked to indicate where on the scale she is "most comfortable" and the "highest level" she experienced during the past week.

The next phase of this exercise involves relaxation and guided imagery. The therapist issues these directions:

I want you to close your eyes, get as comfortable in your chair as you can, and relax. [*For example, have the client do some deep breathing. It is often calming simply to focus as much attention as one can on the pathway of each breath.*] Open your mind's eye to a scene: see yourself being at the highest level you have experienced this past week. Notice what you are doing, who you are with, what you are thinking, how you are feeling. [*Give client a few minutes to experience this level.*] Now, ask yourself: What do I need *to do or think differently* in order to move down one level. Identify what that behavior is for you, and imagine yourself doing it so you can experience the next level down. [*The client is then instructed to repeat this step until she gets to the place where she is most comfortable. If a client's most comfortable spot is high on the out-of-control end of the scale, instruct her to imagine moving down one or two levels, if she can.*]

Once you have reached the level at which you are most comfortable, allow yourself to spend some time at this level. Really pay attention to this comfortable place. What is it like for you? How is it different? What are you doing? What are you thinking? Who are you with? How are you feeling? When you feel you have a clear picture of your comfortable level and have had the time to really experience it and enjoy it, open your eyes.

After this exercise, the client can share any significant realizations about what helped her move from feeling out-of-control to being more comfortable. Following that discussion, it is often helpful for the therapist to ask the client to close her eyes and return, via her imagination, to the comfortable level. This repetition anchors her awareness and clarity of the new behavior.

In using this particular scaling technique, my colleagues and I have observed that most clients note a change in their degree of isolation from others and/or a change to more positive self-talk as fundamental in moving from an out-of-control level to a more comfortable level. In addition, many clients report that this exercise forces them to think about what each end of the scale really means for them. Oftentimes, clients use the phrases "out of control" and "in control" without ever having thought clearly about what these states of being actually entail. Clarifying these terms means that the therapeutic conversation will no longer be using nebulous concepts when these terms crop up. Also, many clients seem to place their comfort level around a 4 or a 5, and this frequently surprises them, since they have often thought that they would need to be at 0, completely in control, in order to be happy.

Therapeutic Letter Writing

Since clients in solution-focused brief therapy are seen only at two- to three-week intervals, it is sometimes helpful to write them brief letters to highlight their progress, reinforce the specific changes they have made, compliment them for the hard work they have been demonstrating, promote hopefulness, and assign an observation task that asks them to pay attention to what they want to see and continue in their lives (deShazer, 1988). Two samples of such letters are shown here.

Dear [Mary]:

I just wanted to drop you a note to let you know how impressed I
am with the changes you have made in such a short period of time.
It really tells me that you are working very hard to make your life
better. I want you to keep doing what you have been doing and to
pay attention to what you want to see continue in your life.

Sincerely,
Barbara McFarland

Dear [Joan]:

I wanted to drop you a note to let you know that I believe things
will get better. At our last session, you seemed a bit discouraged,
and I wanted to assure you that with continued hard work you will
experience some positive changes. Based on my experience with
other clients facing similar concerns, I can tell you that you are
doing extremely well. Your determination to stop binging and
purging is impressive. I want you to keep working and to particularly pay attention to what you want to see continue in your life.
We can discuss your observations at our next session.

Sincerely,
Barbara McFarland

A variation of this task is to have the client write herself a
letter that describes what she wants to be different as a result of
treatment and what she plans to do to make the difference happen. She gives the completed letter to the therapist, and she and
the therapist negotiate the time at which the therapist will mail
this letter to her.

Self-Nurturing Tasks

Many eating disorder clients do not have the ability to self-nurture
or self-soothe. Thus, when faced with an environmental stressor,

their inclination is to self-abuse by binging, purging, exercising, or restricting. The therapist and client must explore exceptions related to the times the client has been able to self-nurture and self-soothe, then employ these exceptions as the basis for ongoing change.

To assist the client to access and reinforce her self-nurturing and self-soothing skills, the therapist gives her this directive: "Between now and the next time we meet, I would like you to pay attention to the times that you are able to nurture or soothe yourself, even if it's just a little bit. Write down in detail when you are able to do this and specifically what you are doing when you nurture yourself. Notice what's different about these times."

The directive is most useful after the client and therapist have had a conversation regarding the importance of self-nurturing skills for all adults as a means of coping with stress. During the follow-up session, the therapist should focus on the exceptions identified and highlight and reinforce the self-care skills the client is already practicing.

Eating Disorders as Resources

The strategy of employing the eating disorder itself as a resource is extremely effective. Like some other valuable strategies, it focuses clients on their beliefs regarding their behaviors. Instead of making interpretations or speculations regarding the role and function of the eating, restricting, or purging behaviors as in traditional therapy, the therapist adopts a line of questioning that teaches both the client and the therapist about the actual function of the eating disorder within the client's reality.

To implement this strategy successfully, the therapist needs to pay close attention to the client's language as she labels her eating disorder. Reviewing EDRC videotapes, my associates and I find that clients typically have key descriptors that they use more than once in discussing their eating problem. For example, clients may refer to their problem as "my bulimia," my focus on food," "this obsession I have," or "my constant thinking about food and weight." The therapist must repeat the client's descriptors in the discussions meant to discover the client's belief's about the eating disorder.

In addition, the therapist must be particularly (and respectfully) curious about the client's reality in relation to the actual benefits of the eating disorder. Using the miracle question and asking the client specifically how she will be different when her self-described eating problem is gone is often a first step in this process.

The second interview question goes like this: "I'm going to ask you a difficult but important question, so take your time. How do you suppose your eating disorder helps or protects you?"

Here are some conversations that demonstrate using the client's language and the miracle question to uncover the benefits of the disorder to the client.

THERAPIST: So on your miracle day, when "your obsessing," your "thinking about food" is gone, what would you notice different?

CLIENT: Well, I wouldn't be thinking about food and thinking how fat I was.

THERAPIST: So what would you be thinking instead?

CLIENT: I would be thinking about my day.

THERAPIST: Yeah? Like what about your day?

CLIENT: . . . Well, about my schedule and what I'll wear that day and what I will be doing at work. I'd work out and then eat breakfast.

THERAPIST: So how will this make your day better?

CLIENT: Well, I'd feel more confident about myself.

THERAPIST: And so what would other people notice different about you when you're more confident?

CLIENT: Well, I'd be more outgoing, talkative, and friendlier. I'd look people in the eye when I talk to them.

The therapist can explore this line of questioning until she or he feels the client has explored it fully. The next phase of questioning then shifts the client from the absence of the problem to a discussion of how the eating disorder has actually helped or protected her.

THERAPIST: I'd like to ask you a rather challenging question. You need to take your time in answering it because it is a very important question. Now, think carefully before answering. In what ways do you suppose this "obsessing about food" has either helped or protected you? [*If the client has difficulty in responding the therapist then says: "You know, in all of my clinical experience, I have found that with many clients the 'obsessing' surfaced initially as a way of really being helpful."*]

CLIENT: Well, I do spend a big part of my day thinking and obsessing about food.

THERAPIST: So in what ways do you suppose this actually helps you?

CLIENT: Well, uh . . . I guess then I don't have to deal with . . . you know . . . my problems.

THERAPIST: So which problems does it distract you from having to deal with?

CLIENT: Well, just stuff like with my boyfriend and the pressures I feel about school.

THERAPIST: So what does this obsessing really help you with?

CLIENT: Well, it . . . I guess . . . it protects me from having to deal with my fear. I really get scared.

THERAPIST: What is it you are scared about?

CLIENT: Well . . . maybe, you know, I'm not sure about whether or not my boyfriend is the right one for me. [*Crying.*] And I guess I'm afraid of failing at school.

THERAPIST: So it sounds like when you start to get scared this obsessing steps in to distract you, . . . do I have that right?

CLIENT: Yeah, that's it.

THERAPIST: So, in a way, you really need this obsessing until you feel you have what it takes to face your fears.

CLIENT: Yeah, I really think so.

THERAPIST: So what would have to be different in order for you to feel more like you could face these fears?

CLIENT: Well, I guess I would have to trust myself more.

THERAPIST: And so how are you different when you trust yourself more?

CLIENT: Well, I listen more to myself.

THERAPIST: When most recently have you listened more to yourself?

CLIENT: I did last week when I trusted I didn't have to exercise one day and I wouldn't get fat.

THERAPIST: How did you do that?

CLIENT: Well, I just told myself that not exercising one measly day wasn't going to make me fat and that I would exercise the next day and I would be all right. [*Laughs*.]

In this case, I continued to discuss this exception with the client and helped her see that she could trust herself more by listening to her self-talk messages. The homework for this type of interview asks the client to look for opportunities to trust herself more (observational tasks).

Here is the way a fourteen-year-old anorexic responded to a similar question about the benefits of her eating disorder.

THERAPIST: I'm wondering how "your anorexia" has surfaced as a way of either helping or protecting you. I know that seems like an odd statement, but I have found that anorexia often surfaces initially as a way of being helpful to the individual. How is this true for you?

CLIENT: Well, I guess it gives me a place to put my feelings.

THERAPIST: Tell me how.

CLIENT: Well, if my anorexia were gone, I wouldn't know what to do with my feelings 'cause I just don't let myself feel things.

THERAPIST: So you really need this anorexia until you feel
more like you would know what to do with your feelings?
Do I have that right?

CLIENT: Yeah. I really do need it right now.

Next, this client and I worked on strategies for helping her need
her anorexia less. We discussed those days she was able to eat more
and then identified how she was expressing her feelings more on
those days. Again, the client was asked to look for opportunities to
express her feelings between sessions.

In another case, the client, a twenty-seven-year-old bulimic,
reported that for a period of five years she had felt in control, done
well, and felt happy with herself. However, in the last six months,
her eating had become increasingly out of control, and she found
herself "focusing much more on food." She was binging on cake,
candy, and pastries—foods she was not interested in during her five-
year exception—and she too was asked how her "focus on food" was
helping her.

CLIENT: I don't really know. I know what you mean though.
[Pauses.] I've always thought of food as pleasure and something that really soothes me.

THERAPIST: So are you saying that you think this focus on
food has surfaced again as way of giving you pleasure and
soothing you?

CLIENT: Well, maybe.

As the client and I explored her five-year exception more fully,
we discovered that during that time she was in nursing school and
was a straight A student, highly respected by both her instructors
and peers. She reported that she felt very much in control during
that time and that she "derived a great deal of pleasure" from achieving her 4.0 grade point average and being very involved in school
activities. Presently, however, it seemed that food was her only

source of pleasure. As she discussed this, she added that she knew that the "pleasure had to come from within and not from without."

I asked her when she had most recently felt this "pleasure within," even if just a little bit. As she pondered this question, she laughed and said that it sure hadn't been in the last six months. Since she had gotten her job, she had felt more and more out of control with food. She also emphasized that her job was extremely stressful and that she did not feel "appreciated or respected."

I asked her again when she had felt this "pleasure within."

CLIENT [*smiling*]: Right before I graduated. Actually, that whole time I was in school, I felt a sense of that pleasure.

THERAPIST: So what do you suppose was different then that you were able to feel it?

CLIENT: I guess I felt better about myself. People at work aren't very nice! [*Laughs.*]

THERAPIST: So what was different that you were able to feel better about yourself?

CLIENT: Well, I understand that having a job and working is very different from being in school. So I don't think I have some unrealistic notion about that. [*Pauses.*] But, you know, as I am thinking about this, the one thing that is very different is that I don't have any time for myself. [*Pauses.*] The one thing that I used to do that I stopped doing was listening to Deepak Chopra tapes. Are you familiar with him?

THERAPIST: Yeah. I really like his philosophy.

CLIENT: Yeah. Listening to his tapes and meditating, . . . especially meditating, really helped me feel that pleasure within. I have been so busy at work and getting my condo decorated that I really haven't made time for me! [*Smiles.*]

THERAPIST: So do you suppose that this focus on food might be a sign that you need to make time for yourself . . . so you can do those things that create that pleasure within feeling?

CLIENT: Yeah! I guess it's been a wake-up call!

The client and I agreed that she needed to get back on track and do more things for herself in order to feel "the pleasure within." She was asked to look for opportunities to feel the "pleasure within," and at the second session, she reported that her eating was less out of control and she had begun meditating for fifteen minutes every morning.

Externalizing Eating Disorders

In working with families, externalizing the eating disorder can also be extremely effective. "Externalizing is an approach to therapy that encourages persons to objectify, and at times, to personify the problems that they experience as oppressive. . . . Those problems that are considered to be inherent, as well as those relatively fixed qualities that are attributed to persons and to relationships, are rendered less fixed and less restricting" (White & Epston, 1990, p. 38).

The following session with a bulimic ("Sandra") and her brother ("Mike"), mother, and father illustrates the effectiveness of this strategy.

THERAPIST: So, Mike, tell me, how would this family be different without this bulimia?

BROTHER: Well, it would be really different. My mother and sister wouldn't be fighting and yelling at each other.

THERAPIST: So what would they be doing instead?

BROTHER: They'd be talking about normal things that other mothers and daughters talk about.

THERAPIST: Like what?

BROTHER: Like about dating and clothes and stuff.

THERAPIST: And so if your mom and sister were talking about normal things, how would you and your dad be different?

BROTHER: I'd want to be at home more. My dad and I, well, we would talk about other things. Right now, that's all we talk about is Sandra and her bulimia and how worried we are.

I asked each family member how things would be different if the "bulimia" were gone, interjecting how powerful the bulimia had become. The father, too, revealed that he and his wife would have other things to talk about if the bulimia were gone, that they might plan a trip together. However, when the therapist asked the mother the same question, after some hesitation and discomfort, she began sobbing and said, "I don't know what I'd do if I didn't have Sandra's bulimia to deal with."

Subsequent sessions focused on how the parents could disempower the bulimia by strengthening their relationship. At the second session, they reported that they were going to take a skiing trip together the following weekend.

Generative Change

In the solution-focused brief therapy model, as has been discussed, change is viewed as generative: small changes lead to larger changes. This principle underlies all the treatment strategies. Thus, rather than looking to eradicate the eating disorder, solution-focused treatment looks to help the client identify an initial step, idiosyncratic to her experience, that leads to one success in altering the problem behavior. The success, in turn, increases her perception of self-efficacy and starts a series of ripples that multiply the initial success into a chain of positive changes.

Rather than engaging in theoretical discussions about the causes of behaviors, the therapist gets the client immersed in the change cycle, using the client's own resources and solution patterns as tools. By facilitating client awareness of what actually works, the therapist guides the client to both an appreciation of her own strengths and an increased faith in her own ability to solve her own problems forever after. By becoming attuned to what is working and her own self-efficacy in making these changes, the client learns a positive view of her ability to manage her eating behaviors.

The strategies and techniques described in this chapter help the client concentrate on actions, behaviors, inner dialogues, and attitudes that ameliorate problem behaviors by attending to those times the behaviors are absent. However, the strategies in and of themselves serve only to make the difference that will get the client unstuck. The therapist's role in follow-up conversations in amplifying, highlighting, and reinforcing what is better, what is different. And what the client needs to keep doing in order to solidify the change is also vital.

Seven

Solution-Focused Group Therapy: A Program Description

"I'm glad they've come without waiting to be asked,"
she thought: "I should never have known who were
the right people to invite!"

—*Lewis Carroll*
Through the Looking Glass

The two major working principles that guide the group program at the Eating Disorder Recovery Center deal with change and hope. We believe that change and success are inevitable, and we believe that personal hope has concrete benefits. This chapter is devoted to a full explanation of the principles and practices in the EDRC group program. The aftercare program and family program at EDRC are also described.

The working principle that change and success are inevitable may encapsulate the most dynamic difference between traditional forms of group psychotherapy and the brief solution-focused form. This principle invigorates group participation. It encourages group members to focus their attention and energies on changes and successes, no matter how small. The norms of the group, therefore, are that "you will succeed" and that "you are capable of doing the hard work needed to achieve your goals." These norms are achievable when the group explores and elaborates on members' exceptions to their problems and the "differences that make a difference" to group members.

As the group becomes attuned to focusing on changes, the generativity of change becomes clearer to the individual group members. Through group discussion and responding to therapist

177

questions, group members become sensitive to the stages of change that they must pass through and the power of the ripple effect. The hope and confidence instilled by this aspect of the group process spill over into group members' other life areas. And group members frequently find resolutions to other problems on their own, by transferring the skills established in the eating disorder group.

As Yalom (1975) suggests, this instillation of hope is one of the major benefits of group psychotherapy. However, my colleagues and I at EDRC see this hope rooted not in client belief in our particular philosophical orientation but rather in the process through which the client identifies, elaborates on, and appreciates her successes, her assets, and her already developed strengths and existing solution patterns. Hope comes from being able to see in oneself the skills and resources necessary to make a change, cope, or solve a problem.

Program Overview

EDRC's group program runs for sixteen weeks. All clients participate in an initial two-hour assessment and orientation session in the first week. For the duration of the program, an hour-and-a-half group psychotherapy session, an hour-and-a-half psychoeducational session, and an hour-and-a-half process group are held once a week. Because the program is individualized, some clients attend all group sessions, while others attend only those relevant to their specific needs. Additionally, clients may, if appropriate, attend up to eight weekly sessions of the Body Image Group, which takes place during the second half of the program.

The EDRC program is open-ended. New members may enter at any time. There are five key aspects to the program.

1. *Screening and pre-treatment orientation.* Pregroup preparation and screening allows clients to know the purpose of the group, its focus, and its parameters before they make a commitment. They can determine whether or not our program can meet their specific needs and/or complement the goals they already have established.

2. *Early establishment of client-determined treatment outcome (client identifies what will be different as a result of treatment)*. At the initial diagnostic interview, the client completes self-reports, including a self-report that answers the miracle question in order to help her identify specifically what she expects to be different in her life as a result of treatment.

3. *Continuous focus on client-directed goals and on treatment progress*. Through self-completed documentation, the client identifies weekly changes, scales herself for progress, and delineates her next level goals. Having a specific focus and format for treatment does not prevent other concerns or conflicts from arising, but it does minimize detours from the client's initial reason for seeking treatment. Most importantly, because of this supportive specific focus and format, clients are often able to see their successes more readily and build on them more rapidly than they would in other contexts. Thus, the group is always oriented toward the present and the future. (Clients who have other concerns emerge during the course of the program and who find that these other concerns disrupt their ability to stay focused on their goals may need to discontinue the group for a time and work with the group therapist individually.)

4. *Maintenance of group cohesion*. Group cohesiveness tends to form fairly rapidly for three reasons. First, everyone has the same basic purpose for being in the group, and group members sense their similarity immediately. Because they have felt so abnormal, isolated, and frequently misunderstood and criticized in daily life, the opportunity to share with others who have had similar experiences stimulates a wave of camaraderie that overshadows their differences. Second, the solution-focused group norms promote conversations that highlight group members' individual resiliencies, solution patterns, and idiosyncratic exceptions. Owing to these norms, group members quickly emulate the therapist's example, readily forming a caring, supporting, trusting environment. They pay attention to what is working and amplify and compliment group members' successes and strengths. Because there is no one

right way to get better, individual empowerment is championed and respect for the individual highlighted. Progress in finding and developing exceptions to problems is accomplished through a variety of mechanisms: verbal interactions, homework assignments, client-reported progress, and in-group exercises.

5. *Preparation for aftercare and identification of posttreatment goals.* Clients are given the opportunity to participate in a six-month aftercare program that prepares them to continue to support the changes they have made. The aftercare program fosters each client's sense of individual responsibility for every aspect of treatment and its outcome, and diminishes concerns over termination from the group, enabling many clients to terminate smoothly and without conflict.

The first and foremost goal of the group program is to increase and strengthen clients' perceptions of self-efficacy and ability to manage their problematic eating behaviors. The program increases clients' awareness of their resources and viable solution patterns, so that they can not only use these abilities to manage their eating disorders but can transfer them to other problem areas. All groups are geared to this end through the major vehicle of the miracle question: "What will be different and better as a result of this treatment experience?"

The documents used in the program reflect these program aspects and goals and include the following:

Self-Report Assessment
Miracle Question Self-Report
Priorities for Treatment
Treatment Plan
Progress in Treatment
Goal Sheet
Orientation/Reflection Sheet
Food Record

Body Esteem Scale

Aftercare Planning: Overall Progress Assessment

Progress in Recovery Assessment

In the remainder of this chapter, I discuss the various steps and sessions in the group program in more detail.

Screening

Regardless of the referral source, an individual seeking services at the Eating Disorders Recovery Center is initially spoken with by telephone. At this time, the prospective client is given basic program information and is screened by a clinical assistant for appropriateness for treatment. If she appears appropriate, she is encouraged to attend a free consultation session and, if she gives her permission, she is mailed a packet of materials about EDRC and eating disorders in general.

During the initial consultation session, the intake therapist describes what eating disorders are, identifies some of the contributing factors in the development of the syndromes, and outlines the specific treatment components of the program and its structure. The individual seeking treatment is encouraged to discuss her specific reasons for seeking treatment, so that she and the therapist can better determine if she is appropriate for the program. If she expresses interest in participating in the program after this consultation, a diagnostic assessment is scheduled.

Assessment

The vast majority of EDRC clients have had periods of success in managing their problematic eating behaviors, either on their own or as a result of other therapy. The assessment process is designed specifically to focus on those successes in order to help the client recognize that she has experienced an absence of the problem and to get her to start seeing the difference that can make a difference, as well as to bolster her sense of self-efficacy. Although her history is gathered, this activity is managed so as not to overshadow the identification and highlighting of current viable solution patterns or strengths. In order to reinforce client responsibility for treatment, we ask the client to complete several documents in this assessment process.

First, she details her miracle day (as described in earlier chapters) by filling out the Miracle Question Self-Report (Resource B).

Second, she identifies her personal priorities and reasons for seeking counseling at this time by completing the Priorities for Treatment form. This form simply provides space for the client to identify her first, second, and third priorities for what she wants to be different as a result of the treatment. It suggests that these priorities might fall in the areas of eating behaviors, exercise activities, self-care/self-nurturing skills, communication skills, the identification and expression of feelings, and so on. She is also asked to use *videolanguage*, meaning that she is to describe how her accomplishing the priority would look if her actions were recorded by a video camera with no sound (O'Hanlon & Wilk, 1987).

Third, the client completes the Self-Report Assessment form (Resource A) that reviews her eating behavior history; medical history; mental health treatment history; alcohol or chemical use history; religious or spiritual attitudes; level of education or vocational training; employment, legal, and financial history; leisure time and recreational activities; and personal strengths and weaknesses. A brief family history and emotional assessment also is completed.

Using the self-report format for this patient history allows us to maintain a present and future focus in the actual therapy sessions. Since the problem-focused questions that appear on the written self-report are separated from the interactive component of the assessment, the client's initial meeting with the intake therapist can immediately delve into the client's miracle day. We believe that this focus is crucial not only in setting the tone for the entire treatment experience but also in orienting the client toward the belief that her complaint is solvable and that she has the resources to solve it herself. The assessment process is designed to communicate that we fully expect the client to make progress and achieve her goals by focusing on a problem-free future. The major objective of the assessment is to help the client crystallize both her exceptions and what can realistically be accomplished as a result of the treatment.

While the client completes the Self-Report Assessment, the intake therapist reviews her Miracle Question Self-Report and Priorities for Treatment form. Then the client takes a break while the intake therapist reviews the various documents in the Self-Report Assessment. When the client and intake therapist get together, the therapist reviews the Miracle Question Self-Report with the client and asks questions to help her depict a highly specific, behaviorally focused Miracle Day. Using the client's responses as her launching point, the intake therapist then interviews for exceptions and previous solution patterns, all of which are documented as they are discussed. The therapist then determines if these exceptions are related to the client's reasons for seeking treatment and works with the client in identifying specific criteria (what will be different) for treatment termination. This information is also documented.

This component of the overall assessment begins the process of encouraging the client to pay attention to what is already going well in her life (deShazer, 1985). In addition, it establishes the tone of treatment—identifying, elaborating, and complimenting the client on what is working.

The documents from the assessment process are used by the staff to develop a written treatment plan. Since the solution-focused model requires that the client determines the goals while the treatment team works collaboratively with her in fulfilling these goals, no treatment goals are included in the treatment plan unless they have been specified for inclusion by the client. The completed plan lists the client's numbered "priorities," from her Priorities for Treatment report, and describes her "goal." It states what the client will undertake to do and also what the treatment staff will undertake to do during the treatment. The EDRC Treatment Plan form also lists the available educational sessions; nutrition groups; body image sessions; individual, family, and couples psychotherapy sessions; and so on, and staff check off the ones that they think would be appropriate for the client. The language of the plan is solution oriented and client based and describes behaviors; staff primarily review goal specificity. Furthermore, this written plan is considered a preliminary and working document that is to be continually revised and modified by the client through weekly completion of further documents.

During assessment, the client also completes a nutritional questionnaire that asks her to rate her levels of nutritional knowledge in several areas, to describe her nutritional concerns, and to note any medical conditions or medications the nutritionist should know about. The nutritionist uses this information in her first assessment meeting with the client.

Finally, all clients are required to have a physical examination and a SMAC-24 blood series, performed either by their physician or by ours.

Although a specific diagnosis is not relevant to our treatment process, we do have to comply with specific licensing and payer requirements. Thus, we do determine a diagnosis of "anorexia," "bulimia," or "eating disorder unspecified," as outlined in the most current edition of the American Psychiatric Association's *Diagnostic and Statistical Manual of Mental Disorders*.

Orientation

The major purpose of the orientation session is threefold:

- Begin the process of reinforcing the awareness of exceptions.
- Gain the client's approval of the treatment plan.
- Have the client sign various administrative documents.

Orientation usually occurs in the hour previous to the first group treatment activity of the day. First, the client completes an

Orientation/Reflections Sheet, writing out what has been better since the diagnostic assessment interview, how the client explains this change, and if nothing has been better, what has been different. After the client has completed this task, the clinical assistant and the client discuss what has been better, so the client can hear the exceptions highlighted and share her reflections on how this happened with the assistant and any other individuals in the orientation group. Taking this time to ask what has been better continues to send the message that change is possible and focuses the client on what is working.

The vast majority of our clients report something as being better since the assessment (this finding is supported by research done by Weiner-Davis, deShazer, & Gingerich, 1987). Clients' reports range from the concrete and behavioral ("I haven't binged") to the more abstract ("I feel hopeful and optimistic because I see coming here as my first step in taking action"). Through the group process, these pretreatment exceptions are refined into more specific and concrete behaviors, and then documented by the client on the Orientation/Reflections Sheet. When actual behavioral changes are reported, clients are encouraged to pay attention to what they did differently and to keep doing those things that seem to make a difference. When changes are more abstract, clients are asked to pay attention to what they did or thought about differently in order to generate their new feelings.

Second, the client reviews the treatment plan, adding personal comments as she desires. Third and finally, she receives a packet of materials pertinent to program participation, such as the program schedule, is informed about emergency procedures, and signs administrative forms, such as a statement of client rights.

Goals and Progress Sessions

The overall purpose of the goals and progress group sessions, of course, is to keep each group member focused on the present and on what is needed in order for her to achieve a problem-free future.

We want her to pay attention to what is better, to exceptions to her problem, and to the attitudinal and behavioral changes necessary to make her miracle day a reality. As I previously mentioned, a majority of clients enter treatment with global ideas of the difference they want ("I want to be light and carefree"; "I don't want to be constantly thinking about food and my weight"), and they frequently lack awareness of the number of small steps necessary to achieve these goals.

In the goals and progress sessions, the client develops this awareness through three specific tasks:

- The refinement of and experimentation with the miracle day
- The review once every two weeks of progress and priorities, using the Progress in Treatment report
- Establishment once every week of goals and a review of goals, using a Goal Sheet

Each client continues to refine her miracle day during two group sessions within the first eight weeks of treatment. In the first session, she reviews her original miracle day description. She reflects on how the miracle is already happening and what changes, if any, need to be made in order for the miracle to be meaningful in her daily life. During this session, she also completes and shares a written revision of her miracle day. Then she is given the coin toss assignment described in Chapters Five and Six, which creates opportunities for her to actively practice her miracle day.

Client observations are discussed in a second session of the goals and progress group, with both therapist and group members highlighting, amplifying, and reinforcing changes that have occurred as a result of the assignment. Any goals that emerge from this group experience are integrated into the client's treatment plan through other components of the goals and progress group sessions.

Typically, the miracle day developed at the assessment, although somewhat refined by the intake therapist, remains fairly general until this first session. Since the miracle day is the basis for goal development, the group sessions must help the client become more specific about the behaviors needed to make her miracle happen. One way these groups are particularly helpful is that they allow clients in the determination or action stages of change to help clients in the contemplation stage become more specific. Because people in the determination and action stages tend to be more behaviorally focused and open regarding successes than clients in the contemplation stage, simply observing and listening to the actors gives the contemplators vicarious experiences of self-efficacy. Subsequently, contemplators frequently experience a reduction of ambivalence and become more motivated to experiment with new behaviors for themselves.

The Progress in Treatment report (Resource C) is used throughout the course of treatment. Clients complete these reports once every two weeks, assessing such aspects of treatment as their changing perceptions of food and weight, their changing body image, and their development of self-nurturing/self-caring behaviors. They also review the priorities they set during assessment and rate their progress using a scaling device on which 1 represents where the client was at the beginning of treatment and 10 represents where she would like to be at the end of treatment; that is, 10 is her picture of her miracle day.

As the client becomes more specific about the attitudinal and behavioral changes necessary to make her miracle day a reality in her daily life, she also becomes clearer about what progress in treatment consists of for her. Typically, clients' initial evaluation of progress is purely sensory. If the client feels she has had a "bad day," she will assess her progress as poor; if she feels she has had a "good day," she will elevate her progress assessment. Such sensory assessments of progress may not be linked to actual behavioral changes at all. By refining her miracle day and assessing her progress biweekly, the client becomes much more knowledgeable about the personal changes that denote progress.

As she reviews her initial priorities and scales her progress, the client also has an opportunity to reflect whether her priorities fit with her miracle day picture. If her priorities are consistent, she will be becoming more focused in her reasons for being in treatment and clearer regarding what she wants to be different as a result of treatment. If a priority is not consistent with her miracle day picture, she has the opportunity to relinquish it or to modify it so that it is more consistent with, and therefore supportive of, her ultimate goal. Reviewing progress also shows the client when she has begun to consistently experience pieces of her miracle day. She is then strengthened in her sense of mastery and self-efficacy, and that awareness, in turn, generates continued practice of the necessary changes.

In addition to the biweekly Progress in Treatment assessments, a complementary Goal Sheet (Resource D) is completed weekly. On these sheets, clients delineate small, specific behaviors they will practice, such as exercising for thirty minutes two times or going out with a friend one time. These small, manageable goals should be relevant to the client's listed priorities. The purpose of establishing such goals weekly is threefold. First, this exercise supports the client in moving from the global to the specific. Second, it heightens her awareness and gives her practice in the behavioral changes necessary to reach her ultimate goal. And third, it helps her determine what she is truly ready to do, what works for her as an individual in contrast to what she has assumed she should do or what others expect from her.

To assist the group members with goal setting and progress assessment, the therapist clarifies and encourages the development of manageable goals. The therapist also has each client consider previous solution patterns and current coping behaviors. And the therapist compliments the client, highlighting and elaborating on successes as the client establishes and reviews goals and assesses progress and priorities.

As treatment continues, goals and progress throughout continue to be determined by the client, not the therapist. The therapist's role is to support the client, revealing and encouraging those behavioral changes necessary to create the change the *client* desires.

Food Groups

Though individuals who struggle with problem eating behaviors often have an expansive knowledge of nutrition, a significant percentage have either misinformation or outdated facts. Consequently, most clients come in clinging to certain myths regarding food, eating, and weight.

The primary objectives of the EDRC food groups are to

- Provide accurate information about food, eating, and exercise, with a focus on helping clients meet basic nutritional needs.

- Provide information about physical activity that improves cardiovascular health and supports emotional and physical well-being, and encourage related goals.

- Develop personal food plans that are unique to each client's life-style and food preferences.

The titles of the various EDRC food group sessions are Evaluating Fats, Fast Foods, and Food Planning I & II. In these sessions, there is no calorie counting, no tracking of food exchanges, no criticizing or cajoling about food intake.

Evaluating Fats teaches clients how to determine the percentages and types of fat intake the body needs to function appropriately. It is a highly effective myth-busting session, as it confronts popular but inaccurate concepts surrounding "fattening foods" and "low-fat" products. This session also elaborates on the usefulness of fat. The United States has become a fat-conscious society, but the downside of that potentially healthy attitude is that many individuals with problem eating behaviors have come to believe that *all* fat is bad. However, individuals who eat virtually no fat rob their bodies of nutrients necessary to function effectively *and* set themselves up for craving for and binging on fats in response to this deprivation.

Fast Foods is another myth-busting session. Eating disorder clients tend to binge on fast foods. The information about fast foods' high fat content and low nutritional value given in this session enables clients to make more informed choices and serves to remove the "good" and "bad" labels from these foods. This session also looks at ways to meet nutritional needs even when consuming fast food.

During the two sessions devoted to food planning, clients develop a healthy food and activity plan based on their own preferences and limitations. The focus is to support the *client in determining for herself* what she is willing to do to change her eating patterns and to specify how she will be able to do this.

A key document for clients in the food group sessions is the food record. It is not unusual for a client to struggle with food records, especially if she has been a chronic dieter. Clients who have kept "food diaries" in the past have frequently used them to count calories or have been required to keep them in order to be accountable to someone else, such as an overinvolved parent or a diet center counselor. To these clients, food records are instruments of criticism, focusing on what is wrong and what needs improvement, rather than instruments of information, highlighting successes related to eating times, portion sizes, and hunger levels.

Respecting the client's right to choose, we encourage but do not require a client to keep and submit food records. Clients are gently reminded at regular intervals how food records can be useful. Once clients recognize the records' usefulness in revealing the problem exceptions of other group members, most clients tend to complete them. The client who does choose to keep food records is encouraged to randomly select two or three days a week for charting and to chart both "good" and "bad" days. That way, client and therapist have a means of reviewing together what was different on good days, not only in terms of foods consumed, but also in regard to exercise or activity, moods, hunger levels, and so on. The food record aids the client to alter her patterns because it heightens her awareness of the overall pattern of her problem eating behaviors and of a specific area she can choose to make different. For example, a client may discover that her most trying time of day occurs when she gets home from work and feels pressured to start supper. This knowledge can help her consider options for managing this time of day differently.

Clients can incorporate their ideas from food group sessions and food records into the weekly Goal Sheet and evaluate the usefulness of the ideas via the biweekly Progress in Treatment assessment, making modifications as appropriate.

Psychoeducational Groups

The psychoeducational component of the EDRC group treatment program is designed to impart information, share concepts, and stimulate client discussion in areas we have come to identify as relevant to clients who choose to participate in our program. Each and every client completes a program evaluation upon termination of treatment, and over our ten-year history, these evaluations have delineated the educational topics clients identify as being most useful and those they would like to see added. These results are used to design this component of the program.

In addition, the psychoeducational group sessions continue the theme and tone of the solution-focused model of treatment, emphasizing to clients that they have the resources, experience, and knowledge necessary to make their lives better; change is inevitable; and change takes hard work and comes in small steps.

The sessions educate clients in three general areas:

- Biobehavioral processes of dieting, purging, restricting, and exercise
- Common cognitive distortions regarding weight, body shape, and food
- Behaviors, personal strategies, and individual resiliencies that create positive change

The psychoeducational sessions are taught through didactic presentations complemented by in-group pen-and-paper exercises and/or scaling and imagery exercises.

The complement in one session entitled The Resilient Self is a series of questions designed to aid the client in reflecting upon and identifying her current resiliencies. This activity is followed by the scaling exercise described in Chapter Five in which the client revisits a time in her life when she has felt empowered and was connected with her resiliencies. She not only reexperiences the empowerment but is also directed to identify details. The act of noting details heightens her awareness of what is different when she feels empowered, allowing her to identify behaviors that will keep her more attuned to her self-efficacy.

As a complement to the Process of Recovery psychoeducational session, each client develops a collage during the session. First, the client reflects on the core questions of the treatment: "What do you expect to be different as a result of being in treatment?" "What will others see different about you when you are finished with treatment?" "What are you willing to do differently?" Then she creates a visual representation of her responses from magazine clips as yet another means of heightening her awareness and generating ideas about specifically how she might make the change she wants happen.

The session entitled Assertiveness includes an activity in which clients form small groups of two or three and each individual has the opportunity to select a situation in which she would like to be assertive and then to role-play that situation with the others, who aid the role-player with coaching and feedback. The client is then encouraged to try out her assertive effort outside of the group and report back in the next session. Again, the client who is in the more active stage of change is frequently able to share her effort with the contemplators so they can experience vicarious success and self-efficacy.

As an experiential complement to the psychoeducational session entitled Contributing Factors, the individual engages in another imagery exercise (also described in Chapter Five), scaling for the cues around problem eating behaviors. Focusing on an experience of daily life, the client is encouraged to pay close attention to what she does and how she thinks regarding different levels of the in-control/loss-of-control continuum. Then, through her imagination, she experiences herself doing something differently, thereby slowly empowering herself to be more in control.

Body Image Sessions

There is much documentation regarding the existence and persistence of a distorted body image among individuals with eating disorders. Our experience at EDRC is that clients' disdain for the body and distortion regarding how the body looks persists even when clients are doing well in other areas of treatment and recovery. It is not uncommon for an individual to experience a relapse in response to a strong contact with her negative body image.

Body image is slow to heal or improve. It is highly susceptible to environmental and internal messages. Virtually all professionals treating problem eating behaviors agree that treatment needs to include ways to help the client develop a more realistic and affirming body image as part of her healthier self-image and self-care strategies. Traditionally, efforts to reach this goal have included imagery exercises designed to help a client uncover the impact of her attitude about the body and, specifically, where her negativity regarding her body originated. But once again, though more subtly than before, these traditional efforts have tended to emphasize identifying what is wrong with the client, rather than exploring client aspects that are functional and affirming.

At one time, EDRC body image sessions followed this traditional vein. With our transition to the solution-focused approach in all other treatment components, our body image sessions have also been restructured so that they aid the client in building on existing fragments of positive attitudes and feelings toward her body and ultimately developing a useful relationship with her body and, consequently, an effective body image. To identify these fragments of positive attitudes, clients are asked to reflect on what they like about their bodies and on those times when they have experienced positive connections with their bodies. Techniques such as guided imagery, writing in journals, group discussion and, on occasion, movement exercises are also employed to uncover positive experiences.

A client working on body image attends eight weekly body image sessions. A process group is conducted every fourth session. Each session has a particular objective or focus.

Session 1: Body Awareness

This body awareness session helps the client begin to develop a heightened understanding of her body, and introduces her to the notion of body image as her mental image of her physical self. Body image is experienced on four levels.

- *Visual:* how the client sees her body
- *Kinesthetic:* how the client feels (tactilely) or senses being in her body

- *Auditory:* how the client talks to her body; the messages she gives herself
- *Intellectual:* how the client thinks about her body, particularly in comparison to the bodies of others, and the judgments she makes

After hearing this information, each client is asked to complete the Body Esteem Scale, on which she rates key body parts and such items as body scent, appetite, physical stamina, reflexes, and weight, stating whether her feelings could be described as acceptance, neutral, or negative. These responses are discussed briefly by the group.

Next, clients perform an exercise to heighten body awareness. They lie on the floor, close their eyes, and relax. The therapist then guides them through a series of activities, such as noticing what parts of their bodies move when they breathe or sensing the contact their bodies make with the floor. Each client is then asked to sense the width of her head, represent that distance with both her hands as she holds them directly over her face, and then gently lower the hands to check the accuracy of her sensing. The client then does the same with her hips. A majority of clients are reasonably accurate in sensing the width of their heads and significantly inaccurate in sensing the width of their hips. Almost always, clients sense their hips to be much wider than they actually are and are surprised by the discrepancy. This experience, then, helps clients understand more fully what is meant by distorted body image. Afterward, each client is given a few minutes to jot down her reflections.

A third component of this first session is a relaxation exercise followed by an activity in which clients scan their bodies to discover where such emotions as peace, love, and hope reside. Once again, group members are given a brief time to write down personal reflections. Each individual is then encouraged to share her experiences with the group as a whole and discussion ensues from the sharing process. Clients commonly say they can find emotions such as love but have more difficulty with emotions such as self-confidence or spirituality. They are assured that this is not uncommon and are encouraged to periodically repeat this activity as they become more attuned with their bodies and emotions.

Session 2: Positive Body Messages

This group session is designed specifically to help the client identify the origins of the positive ways she sees herself and to increase her sense of choice about what her body image can and will be.

As all body image sessions do, this session begins with a brief introduction followed by a period of deep breathing to induce relaxation. Each group member is instructed to make a list of five or six people or groups of people who have had a major positive influence on the development of her body image. From this list, she selects the three whom she feels have been the most influential. The therapist then begins a guided imagery exercise, asking the client to mentally place herself in a quietly pleasant, sun-filled space. One by one, the three influential people she has identified bring her a positive body message to read. She is asked to feel the impact of these messages. To end the imagery activity, the therapist instructs the clients in an affirmation designed to promote acceptance of the positive messages she received. After taking a brief time to write down her reflections, each client shares her experience, if she chooses.

This session has been observed to be the most difficult one for a majority of clients. One client articulated the essence of the difficulty very well, saying, "My first thoughts immediately went to all the negative messages I've received. I really had to push myself to put those aside and remember that there have been some positive messages in my life; that there are people in my life who give me positive messages and accept me as I am." For the client who can recall positive messages despite the difficulty of mentally climbing out of a sea of negativity, a brightness, an optimism, and a change of perspective occurs. Remembering positive comments and taking time to reconnect with a new way of looking at herself frees the client from all-or-nothing perceptions ("I see my body as ugly; everyone sees my body as ugly"). Often, too, the individuals remembered as giving positive body messages are also individuals who were positive to the client overall, that is, they were emotionally supportive, good listeners, and encouraging of client efforts. Consequently, each client reconnects with an array of messages that she can rely on in her efforts to move away from a problem-focused perspective.

Session 3: Miracle Body Image

The miracle body image session encourages each client to identify a time when she felt in harmony with her body and to use this memory to enhance her current relationship with her body.

During the didactic component of this session, the therapist uses a scale of 0 to 10, with 0 representing where the client is today in her relationship with her body and 10 being her ideal relationship with her body. The client is asked to think of the time in her life when she was highest on this scale and to write responses to the following questions:

- Where were you at this time?
- How old were you at this time?
- Who were you with at this time?
- What were you doing? What were some other people doing?
- What specifically about this time created positive feelings about your body and your relationship to it?
- What was different about this time?

After group members complete their responses, the therapist leads the group in a relaxation and then a guided imagery experience. In the guided imagery, each client mentally transports herself back to her time of harmony, visualizing herself and her surroundings, and absorbing the feelings and impressions of this time. After letting this visualization fade, the client is instructed to imagine that a miracle is occurring and that in her present life she somehow experiences the change that creates harmony between herself and her body. She is instructed to visualize the miracle body image as it would occur in her life *today*, paying particular attention to where she is, what she is doing, who she is with, and so on.

Once again, the guided imagery is followed by writing out reflections, sharing the experience, and group discussion. Finally, each client is asked to rate her level of willingness (from 0 to 10) to do anything at all to create a better relationship with her body. If the client ranks herself at midpoint or above on the willingness scale, she is asked to do the coin toss assignment, pretending that she is living in her miracle body on the days the coin comes up heads. If she ranks below the midpoint, her homework for the coming week is to pay close attention to the times when she experiences *any part* of a harmonious miracle body relationship.

In this session, as in session 2, it is sometimes necessary for the therapist to become active and directive in helping the client remember her exceptions. In addition, the therapist must emphasize the phrase *"relationship* with your body." Otherwise, clients tend to think in terms of having their ideal body weight, which is very different from having an ideal relationship with their bodies. If a client is positive she has *never* experienced any degree of acceptance, she is asked to pretend, or imagine, what a harmonious relationship with her body might look like.

Frequently, the time a client will recall was in childhood or another stage of life when she was more carefree and playful, was engaged in fun and rewarding activities, and had a life-style that was not focused on food or weight but on activities and friends.

After the visualization reintroduces her to specific things that have helped her feel better in the past, she has cues for activities or behaviors to pursue in the present. The visualization also reinforces the concept that being problem-focused (obsessing about food, weight, and body appearance) is not what created an affirming body image for her in the past and, therefore, is probably not what will create successful solutions in the present and future.

Session 4: Process

Session 4 consists of a reflecting activity and a visualization that give clients the opportunity to highlight what they have learned so far, specify what has been especially helpful in promoting a positive body image, and identify what they need to keep doing to enhance and maintain a positive body image.

First, each client writes reflections on the following question: "If you were in your miracle body, what would others notice that is different about you?" Group members are asked to be as specific as possible about what other people would see through their actions, activities, and so on.

Then they share their thoughts during an overall group discussion. The client in the contemplation stage (even if she rated her willingness as high), frequently "forgets" the coin toss assignment from the previous session. She will have difficulty identifying what could be different. However, the client in the action stage is likely to complete the coin toss assignment and to have recent experiences that help her know what she does differently on miracle body days and what others notice. By sharing these experiences so others can hear them and the therapist can elaborate on them, she reinforces her own knowledge base and allows contemplators the opportunity to consider possible, workable options.

During the second component of the fourth session, the clients are asked to stand up, close their eyes, and relax. They are then asked to visualize a body image acceptance scale, with the image at

1 representing each client's relationship with her body at the onset of treatment and the image at 10 representing her ideal relationship with her body. Clients are instructed to reflect on the type of body movement they would associate with each relationship (for example, "heavy and plodding" is typical of the low end of the body acceptance scale, "light and fluid" is typical of the high end), and then they are asked to express each type through movement. After this movement activity, they visualize where they are now on the scale; reflect on the type of movement they associate with that rating, and express that movement. The process of integrating visualization and movement supports the client in realizing both mentally and physically what is different when she allows herself a heightened degree of body image acceptance. The acceptance acts kinesthetically to develop a more affirming body image.

Session 5: Positive Body Attitudes

In the Positive Body Attitudes session, each client identifies specific ways she can enhance her positive body attitudes. She writes a list of six to eight words or phrases that describe her positive feelings and attitudes about her body. (She can refer to the positive messages she recalled in session 2 or create new messages.) She then selects the three most powerful and important messages, writes each on a separate sheet of paper, and arranges the sheets in order of ascending importance.

After a period of relaxation, she takes her messages one at a time and uses her imagination to experience what it feels like to be defined in this positive way and how this way of defining herself might affect her daily life (including her relationships, her health, her self-image, and her work). For each defining word or phrase, the client is asked to create a pleasant sensual image (for example, a beautiful sound or a silk scarf) that represents the definition. After doing this with each of her three most important words or phrases, the client is asked to experience all the sensual images together, while paying attention to her emotions and to how her body feels. She is then given an affirmation to enhance the integration of these positive images and the attitudes they reflect.

Again, client response to the session is dependent upon the client's stage of change and how long she has participated in the body image sessions, with contemplators needing more direction from the therapist than actors. Frequently, group participants can be asked to brainstorm some suggestions to assist the client who is having difficulty. Actors, more open to and accepting of the positive messages, will find articulating how this affirmation affects body image and self-image to be a motivator in their efforts to maintain behaviors that enhance their overall self-care and well-being.

Session 6: Body Talk

The purpose of learning body talk is to help group members become aware of how they treat their bodies and begin to develop a healthy mind-body communication system. The session begins with group discussion around the question, "What do you think your body could teach you?"

This discussion is followed by guided imagery in which each client identifies a part of her body she wants to communicate with in a more positive fashion. She is asked to bring her attention to this part of her body, and then to begin to communicate with this part. Initial communication is wordless. The client simply notices any images, associations, or feelings that arise. Then she is instructed to engage in a dialogue that centers on what needs to be different in order for the client's attitude and behaviors with regard to this body part to be more self-nurturing and healthful. The client is also asked to consider her willingness to interact with or treat this body part differently. Upon completion of the guided imagery, the client writes reflections in her journal and then shares them with the group, if she chooses.

What a majority of clients discover during this session (no matter what their individual stages of change) is that the body part most despised needs to be treated differently. It is not inherently "the enemy." Instead, the client's attitudes and behaviors toward it are self-created. This physical aspect of herself is not a separate entity that inflicts harm on her, but a part of herself on which she inflicts harm. Making a choice to change her perspective, therefore, heightens her overall ability to be less negatively obsessed regarding her body and more easily engaged in thoughts and behaviors that promote an overall sense of well-being.

Session 7: The Field of Flowers

The Field of Flowers session helps group members develop the skills needed to neutralize negative thoughts and attitudes which may emerge as they strive to enhance and maintain a positive body image.

Aided by a guided imagery exercise, each client imagines herself in the most beautiful natural spot she can think of. Once in this place, the client is instructed to have an image of herself as the "harmonious you." She is to embrace the harmony and connectedness of all the beauty of this imagined place. An intruder appears in the scene. This intruder is a negative body thought. After considering its form and threat, the client is guided to reach into her power and resources and somehow neutralize the negative thought. After this success, the client is to return to her "harmonious you" experience and consider how it feels to protect and maintain this harmony for herself. She then repeats the process for each negative body thought she realizes through the exercise. As before, after completing the guided imagery, she writes her reflections in her journal and shares them as appropriate.

Actors typically develop creative and enjoyable methods for neutralizing the negative body thoughts (from zapping them with lightning to using magic to make them disappear). Contemplators are more likely to express fear and a sense of powerlessness in the face of their negative body thoughts. However, they are often successful at least at keeping the negative body thought at bay or at imagining something coming along and blowing the negative body thought away, though they are frequently unable to identify what that "something" might be.

Session 8: Process

The eighth session is another processing session. Group members reflect again on the body image acceptance scale and are instructed in the visualization and movement exercise described for session 4.

Because a client may enter the body image series at various points, this session may be the second process group for one client; the first for another. Most often, the client for whom this is the second process group reflects a higher level of body image acceptance and hearing her reflections and observations is helpful for both the client for whom this is the first process group as well as any contemplators. As mentioned previously, even the vicarious experience of success cultivates hope and optimism.

After the client has completed the eight body image sessions, she is once again asked to complete the Body Esteem Scale. Pre- and postsession comparisons and therapist observations indicate that some positive change—acceptance of body parts and functions—occurs through the course of the body image sessions. Many clients note at least a marginal change in those parts or functions despised most at the onset. Notably, the parts originally seen most negatively are the thighs, waist, buttocks, hips, and stomach. These are the areas where women, due to their biology, naturally carry a higher percentage of body fat than men.

Though the client may not have arrived at a high level of acceptance of these body parts, she has gained a greater awareness and understanding of how blaming her body (or these particular parts) perpetuates a negative cycle. As one client commented, "I don't think I'll ever love my stomach, but I understand, now, that talking negatively about it and focusing on it isn't helpful. It just keeps me stuck. If I can just see it as a part of me that needs to be taken care of, just like my skin, or my heart, it takes some of the anger away—and some of the pressure (to have the perfect body) off."

Another important function of the body image sessions is that they continue our focus on moving the client away from the negative and from problem talk. They encourage increasing recognition of what is already positive and what needs to be different.

Psychotherapy Groups

The Psychotherapy group component of the Eating Disorders Recovery Center is intended to synthesize the other aspects of treatment with each client's life experience. The primary and most helpful function of group therapy is the immediacy with which it reduces the isolation and the deep sense of abnormality that the participants generally have been living with.

The major thrust of solution-focused psychotherapy groups is similar to that of all the other groups. Psychotherapy groups

- Identify concerns or complaints shared by the group.
- Explore for each client's exceptions.
- Identify and heighten awareness of each client's previous solution patterns.
- Clarify with each client what needs to be different.
- Assist each client in developing solutions relevant to the here and now.
- Focus on changes in behavior.

The group function is simple and relatively direct. Participants are encouraged to identify and share thoughts, perceptions, and feelings. But at the same time, they are encouraged to look for and acknowledge self-created solutions (pieces of success that exist in what they may be defining as "failure") or to think about what could work for them so their situation might be improved or different. The therapist takes the leadership in directing the tone, complimenting, and elaborating on even the smallest successes, consistently asking, "What's different?" "What's better?"

As individuals spend more time in group sessions, they also become adept at highlighting areas of success for others as well as themselves. This phenomenon, the structure of all the program components, the continuous assessment of progress toward goals, and the fact the treatment experience is time-limited all support the group members in staying focused and solution-oriented.

Although all clients are focused on eating disorders, each client is at a different stage of change and has an individual preference, and these qualities influence the specific individual goals developed. Typically, however, there are also striking similarities. Common concerns beyond the problem eating behaviors typically revolve around assertiveness, interpersonal relationships (particularly parent/child and spousal interactions) and self-esteem. It is not unusual for clients to talk spontaneously about these concerns or other more individual situations such as sexual abuse or job stress. Even when these other concerns are not part of the goals and priorities the client has established for herself, she is often able to apply the resources and solution patterns she is developing to these concerns also.

Psychotherapy groups go through a series of developmental stages just as individual clients do, and the solution-focused group at EDRC is no exception. Because each client enters the group at a different personal stage of change and because individuals continually enter and leave the program, these group developmental stages may not be clear cut, and within a given group, one individual or a small cluster of individuals may exhibit attitudes and behaviors associated with a different developmental stage than the group as a whole. Nonetheless, it is important to be able to recognize each of the four stages and the therapist's corresponding responsibilities.

Stage 1. The client is *problem-focused*. Frequently, she has been attempting to find out why she has problem eating behaviors, and she naturally focuses on the negative, her perceptions of failure, and her "bad" days. The therapist is the most directive at this stage. She or he is mindful of setting the tone by consistently complimenting the client and by elaborating on exceptions and successes, however small. She or he is careful to avoid engaging in problem talk. Though the therapist may *listen* to the client's concerns, her or his *responses* focus on exploring for exceptions and previous solutions or patterns that have been effective. The therapist also reinforces efforts by other group members who support or give feedback to the problem-focused client in a manner that is success- and solution-oriented. At this stage, it may also be necessary for the therapist to be especially verbal in reminding the client of her goals or of previous successes and the solution or patterns she has shared about those successes.

Stage 2. The client begins to become more spontaneous in talking about and *recognizing solutions and exceptions*, both her own and those of other group members. She tends to engage and interact more with other group members, focusing less on the therapist for answers. Her view of herself and her progress toward her goals and priorities leans more to the optimistic and hopeful. She is likely to report some degree of consistently engaging in behaviors she finds useful for reaching her goals.

The therapist continues to be interactive, but is less directive than in the first stage. More time is spent complimenting, amplifying, and reinforcing client-identified changes, as opposed to simply avoiding problem talk. The therapist does not have to be so diligent in helping the client explore for and recognize exceptions or stay so focused on identified goals and priorities.

Stage 3. The client expresses a period of *regression*. She talks about her frustration and anger at having to work so hard and be responsible for making changes. She shows a tendency to return to magical thinking and previously unsuccessful solutions such as dieting, binging, or compulsive exercising. She has difficulty engaging in, and even remembering, behaviors that she identified as helpful in stage 2. Self-doubt surfaces. She questions her own abilities and resources and expresses strong misgivings about the feasibility of her goals.

The therapist's role is to acknowledge the client's frustration and anger, not to empower these feelings but to normalize them, indicating that this regression is a natural stage in the process of change and, therefore, a good sign. Because more of the client's attention now returns to the therapist, she or he must be especially mindful of tone of voice and responses, as in Stage 1.

Stage 4. The client returns to a level of *accepting responsibility* for making changes. She re-enforces her attention on developing and practicing those solutions that move her closer to her goals. She is more spontaneous in recognizing exceptions and successes and is more interactive with other group members than before. She is intent on maintaining useful strategies for her present and future.

The therapist's role returns to that described for Stage 2. Though interactive, she or he is less directive, assuming a role that allows her or him to blend more with the group rather than taking the "expert" role.

A client may certainly experience more than one stage of regression during the course of the sixteen-week program and her subsequent participation in aftercare. The *experience* of regression is, however, not an issue. It is the *response* to the regression that is important. The goal is to help the client reduce her alarm at this slide backward, so she can become refocused. Eventually, the client will come to recognize the normality of regressive periods. This recognition and reduced alarm will combine to allow her to help herself to move out of this stage more quickly.

Aftercare

Upon completion of her individualized course of treatment, each client is eligible to participate in the EDRC aftercare program for six months. The overall purpose of aftercare is to provide an ongoing group experience through which the client can maintain the attitudinal and behavioral changes that make a constructive difference in her daily life and be supported in continuing those changes.

An individual participating in aftercare will contract to attend a specified group at one-week intervals. Each session meets for approximately one and one-half hours. The facilitator may be a member of the treatment team, though when possible a person who has been through the group program and has "graduated" and who has appropriate skills and training may serve as an aftercare facilitator. We believe that using a group graduate as the facilitator (and as an example of success) is an excellent way of supporting clients' perceptions that change is possible and inevitable.

Prior to entering aftercare, the client attends a Discharge Planning Group session with the program therapist, recent program graduates, and people about to complete the program. In this session, the client completes the Aftercare Planning: Overall Progress Assessment (Resource E). She assesses her overall progress and willingness to create change via scaling questions. She describes those behaviors and strategies that she has determined work for her in reaching her goals and maintaining her confidence. Upon completion of the assessment, the client is asked to share her plan with the group. Such sharing frequently generates useful ideas for other group members as well as helping the individual client elaborate on what works for her. The client retains one copy of her Aftercare Planning form and another is retained in the client file.

During the six months of aftercare, the stages of change previously discussed for the Psychotherapy Group will emerge again (particularly stages 3 and 4). The aftercare facilitator's role parallels that of the therapist in the previously discussed stages. As mentioned, however, the client does develop her own ability to recognize and cope with these stages as time goes on.

To further support her goal setting and focus on solutions, once a month the client completes the Progress in Recovery Aftercare Update (Resource F). Via this document, the client continues to highlight what is better, uses a scale to assess overall progress, and determines additional priorities, if any. If a client desires, she can supplement her aftercare experience by using the weekly goal sheets described earlier.

Family Program

Frequently, family members are hesitant about participating in our family program because they think they may be judged and blamed for the client's problem. However, the tone of the EDRC Family Program is consistent with the tone and direction of the other program components. Family program participants are continually encouraged to think about what is helpful, to recognize their own resourcefulness and solution patterns. Blame is a nonissue. The concentration is on identifying solutions, complimenting family members for their willingness to participate in the program, and exploring what is currently working.

The EDRC Family Program is time limited and structured. In addition to its solution orientation, it has these primary objectives:

- Provide factual education about problem eating behaviors.
- Provide education about the general structure and goals of the treatment program.
- Facilitate an increased awareness of exceptions, solution patterns, and personal resources.

- Facilitate group discussion that allows family members or significant others to share thoughts, ask questions, and build hope for successful resolution of their loved one's problem eating behaviors.

- Facilitate group discussion with family members and clients in order to increase communication about exceptions, solution patterns, and client and family resources, and thus develop a viable understanding of what is currently working.

Family program participants are asked to complete a Family Assessment form, and return it prior to or at the first family program session. This document is designed to help family program participants shift from their own tendency to be problem focused by asking them solution-focused questions regarding their significant other. The questions include:

- When are the times your significant other seems to have more control of her eating and/or her purging?

- Identify your significant other's strengths and resources.

- What do you feel you do that is most helpful in supporting your significant other?

- What have you noticed that is different since she started treatment?

- When did you discover that your significant other had concerns regarding her eating, weight, or body image?

- What do you feel your significant other needs most from you at this time?

- Identify what you would like to be different as a result of participating in the EDRC Family Program.

Family program sessions are held once weekly for four weeks. The titles of the first three sessions are Contributing Factors, Am I

Responsible? and Assertiveness and Communication, and these sessions are primarily instructional, presenting information similar to that the clients receive in their psychoeducational sessions. We believe this is helpful because it gives family members and clients a common foundation of information and, therefore, a common ground for sharing with one another.

In addition, family program participants are encouraged to ask their loved ones for specific direction on how best to approach topics such as

- Therapy ("Do you want me to ask you what's going on in your treatment or not?")

- Social occasions ("What types of social occasions are easy? What ones are difficult? What can I do to be helpful at these times?")

- Body image ("Is it helpful for me to compliment you? What ways can I help you promote a more affirming body image?")

- Feelings ("Do you need me to do anything differently when responding or listening to your feelings?")

In the session *Am I Responsible?*, information and discussion focuses on creating a clearer concept of the responsibility unique to each family member and highlighting exceptions and solution patterns for family members. We encourage a redefinition of responsibility, since many family members think themselves responsible for the problem eating behaviors. We present family responsibility as an opportunity to create change for the client. That is, we want "it's my fault my daughter is bulimic" to shift to, "my part in our relationship is to be open to and encourage changes that are useful to my daughter."

Time is taken to encourage participants to identify interactions that they have experienced as successful and to elaborate on the common elements of these times. Suggestions for more helpful attitudes and behaviors are presented upon request. Throughout this session, family members are encouraged to pay attention to what works now and to consider directly asking clients what is helpful to them and what is not.

The fourth session of the family program includes both family members and the respective clients. They all are asked to come to the fourth session prepared to discuss these questions:

- What have you learned?
- What's better; what differences have you observed?
- What do you need from one another?

Throughout the fourth session, participants are encouraged to be specific and detailed, especially in sharing observations and requests. The therapist highlights all improvements noted by participants and helps each family unit determine a specific goal, whether it is simply a continuation of what is working now or is an additional request not previously discussed by the participants with each other.

Solution-Based Program Goals

The EDRC treatment program stresses personal responsibility, the inherent resourcefulness of the client, the exploration of solutions and exceptions to the complaint, and life as an ongoing process of development and change. We do not look to cure the client of her problem eating behaviors, but rather to help her become unstuck at this current point in her life. We recognize that some clients make significant and far-reaching changes in altering their problem eating behaviors, while others make modifications that are much more limited and modest. Some make changes in other areas of their lives yet continue to struggle with their eating behaviors.

From our perspective, it is critical that the client view treatment as serving her needs with a team of professionals who are interested in supporting her goals for change and who are available and helpful. Our program in no way works to repair characterological deficits, challenge resistant or defensive behaviors, or make speculations regarding the client's behaviors, expressed feelings, and/or decisions.

Our program does require action and hard work from participants, yet it respects the individual's particular stage of change in her problem eating behaviors and acknowledges that she may still be at the precontemplation stage at the time of termination. Nevertheless, each and every client is expected to work at changing *something* that would make her life better. This change may or may not, at this point in her life, be the modification of her problem eating behaviors, but it should produce a desired difference of some kind. Additionally, during the course of treatment, the client is free to set her own pace, define her own direction, and do what she needs to do to make her life better.

Eight

Epilogue:
Through the Looking Glass

"Impenetrability! That's what *I* say!"

"Would you tell me, please," said Alice, "what
that means?"

. . . "I meant by 'impenetrability' [said Humpty
Dumpty] that we've had enough of that subject, and
it would be just as well if you'd mention what you
mean to do next, as I suppose you don't mean to stop
here all the rest of your life."

—*Lewis Carroll*
Through the Looking Glass

The fourth wave of clinical influence brings to the field of eating
disorders a paradigm that allows for the ongoing discovery of client
possibilities that are idiosyncratic to each client's experience.
Solution-focused brief therapy is transforming this therapeutic field.
Clinicians are learning to ignore causality, to look beyond labels in
order to explore and appreciate the reality and unique needs of each
individual client. Solution-focused therapy transmutes the therapeutic relationship from a hierarchy to a collaboration. This new
partnership between client and therapist views the client as capable
and competent and as an expert in her own care. In this fourth
wave of clinical influence, therapy views the change process as
natural, ongoing, and generative. Further, therapy focuses on the
accomplishment of client-directed, specific, salient, and achievable
goals. Perhaps the fourth wave's greatest contribution is that it
places responsibility for change on the client.

I hope that this book has expanded the mindfulness of clinicians who treat eating disorder clients, as well as providing these clinicians with some basic tools for applying the solution-focused model of brief therapy with their clients. According to Langer (1989), being mindful—that is, open to new perspectives and new information—does not require any real effort: however, "what may take effort is the transition from a mindless to a mindful mode just as in physics effort is required to put a still body into motion." (p. 201).

In my experience, this transition initially requires patience and persistence and unfolds in three stages, the first two of which are action based. In the first stage, the clinician acquires the necessary clinical education by participating in formal solution-focused training opportunities. In the second stage, the clinician begins to implement solution-oriented strategies. This initial doing of solution-focused work requires much practice and discipline. There is great labor in refraining from making speculations, interpretations, and assumptions about the client, her verbalizations, and her presenting symptoms. Instead of traversing dark tunnels and labyrinths of pain and dysfunction, the solution-focused therapist must access client strengths and resources and employ them in the formation of a viable and meaningful solution.

In the third stage, the clinician experiences a gradual, almost imperceptibly increasing wave of energy, which not only gives more momentum to her or his creativity and mindfulness but also shapes a new perspective about therapy, the role of the therapist, the eating disorder client, and the change process itself. This third stage is characterized by an attitude of simple respect for the individual client's inherent desire to be well and to live well.

Throughout both my clinical and consulting work, it is clear to me that clients are currently undergoing a transition in their own mindfulness regarding therapy and its benefits. They are becoming increasingly vocal regarding their need to have briefer, more goal-specific treatment that focuses on the present and the future. They are less concerned with understanding the origins of their discomfort and more interested in discovering ways to make things better and get on with the business of living their lives.

The solution-focused model may very well be replaced by other models some day, but the fifth wave, whatever it may evolve to be, is sure to continue to function within the paradigm of health, wellness, and human possibility that the fourth wave has introduced.

Given the tenacity of compulsive eating, purging, or restricting behaviors, eating disorder clients are prone to relapses. Therefore, therapists need to ask just what they want the client to leave her treatment with. Should she leave with a mindset that promotes ongoing attempts at insight into a never-ending problem and the belief that a cure will come with the magical key of understanding? Or should she depart with a mindset that promotes her belief in her resources to manage her eating behavior and other challenges that life presents?

I have come to recognize that by shifting the underlying paradigm of therapy from disease to health we clinicians make it possible for the eating disorder clients we treat to achieve, more than anything else, an increased sense of self-efficacy which empowers them to face other life challenges. As we continue to attend to what is *inside* the client that is good, worthwhile, capable, and competent, the client becomes more connected to these qualities within herself. She is empowered to believe in her own ability to manage her life. And she is then able to see far beyond the looking glass.

Resource A:
Assessment Tools

Name: _____

Date: _____

Mental Health Treatment History

1. Please list any previous psychiatric treatment including the following information: inpatient or outpatient; name of therapist; dates of treatment; medications taken.

2. Are you currently involved in any form of counseling? (If yes, specify with whom.)

3. Are you currently using any medications for depression, anxiety, stress, and or similar conditions? (If yes, What are they? Who is monitoring/prescribing them for you?)

Alcohol/Chemical Use

Have you used any of these substances in your lifetime?

Substance	Amount	Frequency
Alcohol (beer, wine, liquor)		
Tranquilizers (Valium, Librium, Xanax)		
Cocaine		
Barbiturates (Seconal, Tuinal)		
Sleeping pills (Halcion, Dalmane)		
Hallucinogens (LSD, PCP)		
Pain pills (Darvon, Ralwin, Darvocet)		
Stimulants (amphetamines, speed)		
Narcotics (codeine, percodan, heroin, Demerol)		
Marijuana		
Others		

1. Have you ever had substance abuse treatment? (If so, when, where, with whom?)

2. Do you now or have you ever felt you had a problem with drugs or alcohol?

3. Comments:

Educational/Vocational Training Assessment

1. What is your educational background?
   (Describe the experience.)
2. Describe any educational goals you may have at this time.

Employment/Legal/Financial Assessment

1. What is your employment history? (Describe types of work, attitudes toward work, reasons for leaving jobs.)

2. Describe how you feel about your current job. Do you feel your eating patterns (or your weight) have interfered with job performance or promotion?

3. Do you consider yourself to have financial problems at this time (particularly any problems related to treatment or to money spent in relation to compulsive behavior)?

4. Have you had any legal problems?

Strengths Assessment

1. Describe three of your strengths. Be specific about how they help you in your daily life.

2. List three things that you would like to improve about yourself. Do *not* include your appearance in this list.

Leisure Time/Recreational Activity Assessment

1. Please indicate activities or interests that you enjoy, such as, hobbies, sports, or other leisure time pursuits.

2. Do you feel you have any particular talents or skills that you are not currently using to their full potential? (Please describe them.)

3. Do you feel that your current problem/concern has affected your ability to use your leisure time and talents? (If so, please explain.)

Social Assessment

1. Describe how it was to grow up in your family. Be sure to include issues related to how discipline was handled, how feelings were dealt with, how losses were dealt with, any incidences of sexual abuse, economic status, and significant physical and/or emotional illnesses.

2. Has anyone in your family ever received treatment for psychiatric problems, alcoholism, other addictive behaviors, or other concerns?

3. If no one has ever received any such treatment, in your estimation is there anyone who should have received treatment?

4. Are you currently married or involved in any long-term relationship? If so, describe this relationship.

5. Do you have any children? If yes, describe them.

6. Identify any previous marriages or long-term, significant relationships. Note reason for separation/divorce.

7. Describe your current support system. Include personal relationships as well as support groups.

8. Describe your first sexual encounter.

9. Please describe your most recent or current sexual involvement. What conflicts and considerations exist due to this involvement?

10. Please describe any incidents of sexual abuse you have experienced.

Emotional Assessment

Have you ever experienced any of the following? If so, describe the situation.

_____ Suicidal thoughts _____

_____

_____

_____

_____Attempted Suicide _____

_____

_____

_____

_____Depression _____

_____

_____

_____

_____Severe anxiety _____

_____

_____

_____

_____Explosive episodes _____

_____

_____

_____

On a scale of 0 to 10 (with 0 being not at all and 10 being severe), how would you rate yourself currently?

_____Suicidal thoughts

_____Depression

_____Anxiety

_____Explosive episodes

Religious/Spiritual Assessment

1. Discuss your religious background and its effects positive and negative (if any) on your growth and development.
2. What are your beliefs about religion and/or spirituality currently?
3. Do you feel religion or spirituality is an important aspect of your life?
4. Do you feel there are any obstacles to your spiritual/religious growth at this time?

Medical History Self-Report

1. Height_____ Weight_____ Blood pressure_____

2. Have you gained/lost more than 10 lbs. in the past year?
   _____Yes _____No. If yes, how much? _____

3. What is your lowest and highest weight since age 23?
   Lowest_____ Highest_____

4. Do you have a history of or currently have a significant
   medical condition? _____Yes _____No

   If yes:

   What condition? _____

   When was it diagnosed? _____

   How was it treated? _____

   What condition? _____

   When was it diagnosed? _____

   How was it treated? _____

5. Does your family have a history of:

   _____Heart disease

   _____Diabetes

   _____Strokes

   _____Thyroid disorders

   _____Cancer

   _____Obesity

   _____Anorexia

   _____Bulimia

6. List all medications you take and how often and state why you take each one.

Medication	How Often	Why Taken
_____	_____	_____
_____	_____	_____
_____	_____	_____
_____	_____	_____
_____	_____	_____

7. Have you had any abnormal blood test? ___Yes ___No
   If yes:

Abnormal Blood Test	Date (Approximate)
_____	_____
_____	_____
_____	_____

8. Do you follow a modified diet for health reasons?
   _____Yes _____No
   If yes:

   _____Diabetic

   _____Low sodium (salt)

   _____Low cholesterol

   _____Hypoglycemic

   _____Low fat

   _____Other

9. Do you currently:

_____Binge

_____Vomit

_____Take laxatives

_____Take diet pills

_____Take water pills

_____Exercise excessively

10. Have you ever routinely:

_____Binged

_____Vomited

_____Taken laxatives

_____Taken diet pills

_____Taken water pills

_____Exercised excessively

Eating History

1. Height_____   Weight_____

2. Have you gained/lost more than 10 lbs. in the past year?
   If yes, how much: _____

3. What was your lowest and highest weight in the past 5 years?
   Lowest_____   Highest_____   Current_____

4. Describe problems you are currently having with food/weight
   (include eating patterns, distorted body image, purging, fear,
   guilt)._____

   _____

   _____

   _____

   _____

5. At what age did you begin having problems with food/weight?
   Describe the situation. _____

   _____

   _____

   _____

   _____

6. At what age did you go on your first diet?

   _____

   _____

   _____

7. How have you tried to control your compulsive eating and/or
   weight? Identify any treatment or structured programs in
   which you have participated (for example, psychotherapy,
   hypnosis, Weight Watchers, fad diets, and so on).

   _____

   _____

   _____

   _____

8. While compulsively eating, have you:

_____Sneaked

_____Hidden

_____Stockpiled

_____Stolen

_____Lied

_____Eaten alone

_____Eaten before eating in public

_____Eaten very rapidly

Please describe the situation.

_____

_____

_____

_____

9. Are you able to tell when you are physically full? _____
Are you able to tell when you are physically hungry? _____
Do you eat when you are full or when you are not
hungry? _____

10. How have you acquired your knowledge of nutrition?

_____Through books (list titles)

_____

_____

_____From a nutritionist

_____Through attending classes or programs (which ones)

_____

_____

_____Other (be specific)

_____

_____

11. Indicate your level of knowledge of each topic.

A. Portion size

_____I have adequate information

_____I have basic information but would like a review

_____I need more information

_____Other _____

_____

_____

Comments: _____

_____

_____

B. Fat content of foods

_____I have adequate information

_____I have basic information but would like a review

_____I need more information

_____Other _____

_____

_____

Comments: _____

_____

_____

C. Nutrition needs (Pyramid based)

_____I have adequate information

_____I have basic information but would like a review

_____I need more information

_____Other _____

_____

D. Meal Planning

_____I have adequate information

_____I have basic information but would like a review

_____I need more information

_____Other _____

_____

12. Does your family have a history of:

_____Heart disease

_____Diabetes

_____Stroke

_____Thyroid disorders

_____Cancer

_____Obesity

_____Anorexia

_____Bulimia

13. Indicate any of the following that currently apply to you.

_____Pregnancy

_____Diabetes

_____Hypoglycemia

_____Hypo- or hyperthyroidism (indicate which one)

_____

_____Heart disease

_____Hyperlipidemia

_____High cholesterol

_____Vegetarianism

_____Food allergies

_____Any other medical concerns (list)

_____

_____

14. Please list any medications you take routinely or have taken routinely in the past year.

_____

_____

15. Do you currently:

_____Binge: ____(number of times weekly)

_____Vomit: ____(number of times weekly)

_____Take laxatives

_____Take diet pills

_____Take water pills

_____ Exercise excessively _____(number of times weekly for _____ hours)

16. Have you ever routinely:

_____Binged

_____Vomited

_____Taken laxatives

_____Taken diet pills

_____Taken water pills

_____Exercised excessively

17. Is there anything else you would like to discuss with the nutritionist? If so, please indicate.

_____

_____

_____

_____

Thank you for your cooperation.

Nutritionist feedback:

_____

_____

_____

Resource B:
Working with the Miracle Question

Name: _____

Date: _____

Instructions. Please read the following questions and answer them as completely as you can, including as many specific details as possible. Keep in mind that feelings often influence actions. In completing the following, consider how your feelings (internal experiences) *and* your actions (external behaviors) would be different from what they are now. Particularly when completing the question regarding your miracle day, it is important to include *both* how you will feel different and (as a result) what you would *do* differently or what others would *observe* as different about you.

1. Imagine that when you go to sleep tonight, sometime during the night while you are sleeping, a miracle occurs. All the problems that brought you to the Eating Disorders Recovery Center are solved. When you wake up tomorrow, what would your "miracle day" be like? (Describe this miracle day with as much specific detail as you can.)

2. Who would be the first person to notice something different about you? What would he or she notice? (Remember, people cannot see your internal experiences. Focus on what he or she would observe that is different in your behaviors.)

3. Who else would notice something different about you? What would these individuals notice?

4. If no one else would notice something different about you, what would *you* notice different about yourself?

5. Using the following scale, with 10 being your miracle day and 1 being the furthest away from your miracle day, what is the closest to your miracle day you have ever gotten in the last year?

Furthest from
Miracle Day   Miracle Day

---

1   5   10

6. Describe the time identified in the previous question in detail. Include who you were with, what he or she noticed that was different about you, when it was and where you were, and what you were doing and why you were doing it.

7. Using the same scale (10 is your miracle day, 1 is furthest away from your miracle day), where are you today?

Furthest from
Miracle Day   Miracle Day

---

1   5   10

8. Explain how you have managed to achieve this level. (Be specific.)

9. What do you want to be different by the time your treatment is finished?

10. What would be the first, smallest sign that would tell you that you have achieved your goal?

11. Using the following scale (10 being very willing and 1 being not very willing), how willing are you to make the changes necessary to achieve your goals?

Not Very   Very
Willing   Willing

---

1   5   10

Resource C:
Progress in Treatment

Name: _____

Date: _____

1. What has been better this past week in your eating, exercising, and/or self-nurturing/self-caring? (Be specific.)

   What was better about your eating?

   If nothing was better, what was different?

   What was better about your exercising?

   If nothing was better, what was different?

   What was better about your self-nurturing/self-caring?

   If nothing was better, what was different?

2. What have *you* or *others* noticed that is different about you this past week? (Be specific.)

3. On the following scale (with 1 being where you were at the beginning of treatment and 10 being where you would like to be at the end of treatment), where are you *today* regarding your relationship to food, your feelings about your weight, and your body image? (Use *F* to indicate food, *W* to indicate weight, and *B* to indicate body image.)

Beginning of   End of
Treatment   Treatment

1   5   10

4. What are you doing to stay at this level?
   (Be specific in each area.)

   Food:

   Weight:

   Body image:

5. What would you have to do to move up one level?
   (Be specific in each area.)

   Food:

   Weight:

   Body Image:

6. On a scale of 1 to 10, rate your progress in each area you
   identified as a priority for yourself in treatment, with 1 being
   no progress and 10 being *progress completed, problem resolved.*

   Priority 1: _____

   ____ 1–10 rating

   What did you do to get to this level?
   Do you wish to move up one level? ____Yes ____No
   If yes, what do you need to do to move up one level?

   Priority 2: _____

   ____ 1–10 rating

   What did you do to get to this level?
   Do you wish to move up one level? ____Yes ____No
   If yes, what do you need to do to move up one level?

   Priority 3: _____
   ____ 1–10 rating

   What did you do to get to this level?
   Do you wish to move up one level? ____Yes ____No
   If yes, what do you need to do to move up one level?

7. Would you like to change or modify your priorities in any way?
   If so, please indicate how.

8. Is there anything you wish to communicate to your therapists? Please make your comments here.

Patient signature: _____

Date: _____

Therapist signature: _____

Date: _____

Resource D:
Goals

Name: _____

Date: _____

This next week, I will maintain or further my progress in treatment by setting goals in some or all of the following areas. (Please describe specific goals.)

Eating behavior:

Exercise:

Self-nurturing:

Other:

Return this goal sheet next week!

Resource E:
Aftercare Planning

Name: _____

Date: _____

Instructions. In responding to the following questions, consider your overall progress since entering treatment and where you want to be by the end of treatment.

1. On the following scale (with 1 being where you were at the beginning of treatment and 10 being where you would like to be at the end of treatment), where are you *today* regarding your relationship to food, your feelings about your weight, and your body image? (Use *F* to indicate food, *W* to indicate weight, and *B* to indicate body image.)

Beginning of Treatment		End of Treatment
1	5	10

2. What did you do to get to this level? (Be specific.)

3. How confident are you that you can stay at this level?

Not Very Confident		Very Confident
1	5	10

* If your confidence level is 4 or below, please skip item 4 and complete item 5. If your confidence level is 5 or above, please complete item 4 and skip item 5.

4. If your confidence level is 5 or above, what do you need to do to move up one level? (Be specific.)

5. If your confidence level is 4 or below, what do you need to do to maintain your current level of confidence?

6. On the following scale (with 1 being where you were at the beginning of treatment and 10 being where you would like to be at the end of treatment), where are you *today* in relation to exercise?

Beginning of   End of
Treatment   Treatment

---

1   5   10

7. What did you do to get to this level? (Be specific.)

8. How confident are you that you can stay at this level?

Not Very   Very
Confident   Confident

---

1   5   10

* If your confidence level is 4 or below, please skip item 9 and complete item 10. If your confidence level is 5 or above, please complete item 9 and skip item 10.

9. If your confidence level is 5 or above, what do you need to do to move up one level? (Be specific.)

10. If your confidence level is 4 or below, what do you need to do to maintain your current level of confidence?

11. On the following scale (with 1 being where you were at the beginning of treatment and 10 being where you would like to be at the end of treatment), where are you *today* regarding your self-nurturing/self-care?

Beginning of   End of
Treatment   Treatment

---

1   5   10

12. What did you do to get to this level? (Be specific.)

13. How confident are you that you can stay at this level?

Not Very   Very
Confident   Confident

1	5	10

  * If your confidence level is 4 or below, please skip item 14 and complete item 15. If your confidence level is 5 or above, please complete item 14 and skip item 15.

14. If your confidence level is 5 or above, what do you need to do to move up one level? (Be specific.)

15. If your confidence level is 4 or below, what do you need to do to maintain your current level of confidence?

16. If this applies to you, on the following scale (with 1 being where you were at the beginning of treatment and 10 being where you would like to be at the end of treatment), where are you *today* regarding your spiritual recovery?

Beginning of   End of
Treatment   Treatment

1	5	10

17. What did you do to get to this level? (Be specific.)

18. How confident are you that you can stay at this level?

Not Very   Very
Confident   Confident

1	5	10

  * If your confidence level is 4 or below, please skip item 19 and complete item 20. If your confidence level is 5 or above, please complete item 19 and skip item 20.

19. If your confidence level is 5 or above, what do you need to do to move up one level? (Be specific.)

20. If your confidence level is 4 or below, what do you need to do to maintain your current level of confidence?

21. On the following scale (with 1 being where you were at the beginning of treatment and 10 being where you would like to be at the end of treatment), where are you *today* regarding your emotional recovery?

Beginning of Treatment		End of Treatment
1	5	10

22. What did you do to get to this level? (Be specific.)

23. How confident are you that you can stay at this level? What would you have to do to move up one level?

Not Very Confident		Very Confident
1	5	10

* If your confidence level is 4 or below, please skip item 24 and complete item 25. If your confidence level is 5 or above, please complete item 24 and skip item 25.

24. If your confidence level is 5 or above, what do you need to do to move up one level? (Be specific.)

25. If your confidence level is 4 or below, what do you need to do to maintain your current level of confidence?

26. What have others noticed is different about you since you began treatment? (Answer for each group.)

    Immediate family:

    Friends:

    Co-workers:

27. In each area you identified as a priority for you in treatment, rate your progress from 1 to 10 with 1 being *no progress* and 10 being *progress completed, problem resolved.*

    Priority 1:_____

    ____1–10 rating

    What did you do to get to this level?

    Do you wish to move up one level? ____Yes ____No

    If yes, what do you need to do to move up one level?

    Priority 2:_____

    ____1–10 rating

    What did you do to get to this level?

    Do you wish to move up one level? ____Yes ____No

    If yes, what do you need to do to move up one level?

    Priority 3:_____

    ____1–10 rating

    What did you do to get to this level?

    Do you wish to move up one level? ____Yes ____No

    If yes, what do you need to do to move up one level?

28. Would you like to change or modify your priorities in any way? If so, please indicate how.

29. What do you need to do to make progress on this new priority?

Patient signature: _____

Date: _____

Therapist signature: _____

Date: _____

Resource F:
Progress in Recovery

Name: _____

Date: _____

1. What has been better this past month in your eating, exercising, and/or self-nurturing/self-caring? (Be specific.)

    What was better about your eating?

    If nothing was better, what was different?

    What was better about your exercising?

    If nothing was better, what was different?

    What was better about your self-nurturing/self-caring?

    If nothing was better, what was different?

2. What have *you* or *others* noticed that is different about you since you began in recovery? (Be specific.)

3. On the following scale (with 1 being where you were at the beginning of treatment and 10 being where you would like to be at the end of treatment), where are you *today* regarding your relationship to food, your feelings about your weight, and your body image? (Use F to indicate food, W to indicate weight, and B to indicate body image.)

Beginning of   End of
Treatment   Treatment

---

1   5   10

4. What are you doing to stay at this level?
   (Be specific in each area.)

      Food:

      Weight:

      Body image:

5. What would you have to do to move up one level?

      Food:

      Weight:

      Body Image:

6. Do you have any additional priorities in your personal recovery at this time? If so, what are they? What is helping you deal with them effectively? (Be specific.)

7. Is there anything you wish to communicate to your aftercare facilitator? (Explain.)

Patient signature: _____

Date: _____

Therapist signature: _____

Date: _____

References

Anderson, H., & Goolishian, H. (1988). Human systems as linguistic systems: Preliminary and evolving ideas about the implications for clinical theory. *Family Process, 27*(4), 371–393.

Bandura, A. (1977). Self efficacy: Towards a unifying theory of behavioral change. *Psychological Review, 84,* 191–215.

Bandura, A. (1982a). The self and mechanisms of agency. In J. Suls (Ed.), *Psychological perspectives on the self* (Vol. 1, pp. 1–39). Hillsdale, NJ: Erlbaum.

Bandura, A. (1982b). Self-efficacy mechanism in human agency. *American Psychologist, 37,* 122–147.

Bateson, G. (1972). *Steps to an ecology of mind.* New York: Ballantine Books.

Berg, I. K. (1992). Solution focused brief therapy. Training workshop conducted at Dayton, OH.

Berg, I. K., & Miller, S. (1992). *Working with the problem drinker.* New York: W.W. Norton.

Bloom, B. (1981). Single session therapy: Initial development and evaluation. In S. Budman (Ed.), *Forms of brief therapy.* New York: Guilford Press.

Boskind-Lodahl, M. (1976). Cinderella's stepsisters: A feminist perspective on anorexia nervosa and bulimia. *Signs: Journal of Women in Culture and Society, 2,* 342–356.

Browning, W. (1985), Long-term dynamic group therapy with bulimic patients: A clinical discussion. In S. Emmett (Ed.), *Theory and treatment of anorexia nervosa and bulimia* (pp. 141–153). New York: Brunner/Mazel.

Bruch, H. (1970). Family background in eating disorders. In E. Anthony & C. Kouperik (Eds.), *The child in his family* (pp. 207–224). New York: Wiley.

Bruch, H. (1973). *Eating disorders: Obesity and anorexia nervosa.* New York: Basic Books.

Bruch, H. (1977). Psychotherapy in eating disorders. *Canadian Psychiatric Association Journal, 22*(3), 102–108.

Bruch, H. (1978). *The golden cage.* Cambridge, MA: Harvard University Press.

Bruch, H. (1985). Four decades of eating disorders. In D. Garner & P. Garfinkel (Eds.), *Handbook of psychotherapy for anorexia nervosa and bulimia* (pp. 7–18) New York: Guilford Press.

Brumberg, J. (1988). Fasting girls: The emergence of anorexia nervosa as a modern disease. Cambridge, MA: Harvard University Press.

Budman, S., & Gurman A. (1988). Theory and practice of brief therapy. New York: Guilford Press.

Cade, B., & O'Hanlon, W. (1993). A brief guide to brief therapy. New York: W.W. Norton.

Cash, T., Winstead, B., & Janda, L. (1986, December). Body image survey report: The great American shape-up. Psychology Today, pp. 30–37.

Cohler, B. (1977). The significance of the therapist's feelings in the treatment of anorexia nervosa. In S. Feinstein & P. Giovacchini (Eds.), Adolescent psychiatry (Vol. 5, pp. 352–384). New York: Jason Aronson.

deShazer, S. (1984). The death of resistance. Family Process, 23, 79–93.

deShazer, S. (1985). Keys to solution in brief therapy. New York: W.W. Norton.

deShazer, S. (1988). Clues: Investigating solutions in brief therapy. New York: W.W. Norton.

deShazer, S. (1990). What is it about brief therapy that works? In J. Zeig & S. Gilligan (Eds.), Brief therapy: Myths, methods, and metaphors (pp. 90–99). New York: Brunner/Mazel.

deShazer, S. (1991). Putting difference to work. New York: W.W. Norton.

deShazer, S., & Berg, I. (1985). A part is not apart: Working with only one of the partners present. In A. Gurman (Ed.), Casebook of marital therapy (pp. 212–233). New York: Guilford Press.

deShazer, S., & Berg, I. (1993). Making numbers talk: Language in therapy. In S. Friedman (Ed.), The new language of change (pp. 5–24). New York: W.W. Norton.

deShazer, S., Berg, I., Lipchik, E., Nunnally, E., Molnar, A., Gingerich, W., & Weiner-Davis, M. (1986). Brief therapy: Focused solution development. Family Process, 25, 207–219.

DiClemente, C. (1991). Motivational interviewing and the stages of change. In W. Miller & S. Rollnick (Eds.), Motivational interviewing (pp. 191–202). New York: Guilford Press.

DiClemente, C., Prochaska, J., & Gibertini, M. (1985). Self efficacy and the stages of self-change in smoking. Cognitive Therapy and Research, 9, 181–200.

Dolan, Y. (1992). Resolving sexual abuse: Solution focused therapy and Ericksonian hypnosis for adult survivors. New York: W.W. Norton.

Erickson, M. H. (1954a). Pseudo-orientation in time as a hypnotic procedure. Journal of Clinical and Experimental Hypnosis, 2, 261–283.

Erickson, M. H. (1954b). Special techniques of brief hypnotherapy. Journal of Clinical and Experimental Hypnosis, 2, 109–129.

Erickson, M. H. (1965). The use of symptoms as an integral part of hypnotherapy. American Journal of Hypnosis, 8, 57–65.

Erickson, M. H., & Rossi, E. L. (1981). Experiencing hypnosis. New York: Irvington.

Fahy, T., & Eisler, I. (1993). Impulsivity and eating disorders. *British Journal of Psychiatry, 162,* 193–197.

Fisch, R., Weakland, J. H., & Segal, L. (1982). *The tactics of change: Doing therapy briefly.* San Francisco: Jossey-Bass.

Friedman, S. (1992). Constructing solutions (stories) in brief family therapy. In S. Budman, M. Hoyt, & S. Friedman, (Eds.), *The first session in brief therapy* (pp. 282–305). New York: Guilford Press.

Friedman, S., & Fanger, M. (1991). *Expanding therapeutic possibilities: Getting results in brief therapy.* Lexington, MA: Lexington Books.

Furman, B., & Ahola, T. (1992). *Solution talk: Hosting therapeutic conversations.* New York: W.W. Norton.

Garfield, R. (1971). Research on client variables in psychotherapy. In S. Garfield & A. Bergin (Eds.), *Handbook of psychotherapy and behavior change* (pp. 271–298). New York: Wiley.

Garfield, R. (1978). Research on client variables in psychotherapy. In S. Garfield & A. Bergin (Eds.), *Handbook of psychotherapy and behavior change* (2nd ed., pp. 213–256). New York: Wiley.

Garfinkel, P. (1974). Perception of hunger and satiety in anorexia nervosa. *Psychological Medicine, 4,* 309–315.

Garner, D. (1986). Cognitive therapy for anorexia nervosa. In K. Brownell & J. Foreyt (Eds.), *Handbook of eating disorders* (pp. 301–327). New York: Basic Books.

Garner, D. (1987). Psychotherapy outcome research with bulimia nervosa. *Psychotherapy Psychosomatics, 48,* 129–139.

Gilligan, S. (1990). Coevolution of primary process. In J. Zeig & S. Gilligan (Eds.), *Brief therapy: Myths, methods, and metaphors* (pp. 359–377). New York: Brunner/Mazel.

Haley, J. (1967). Commentary on the writings of Milton H. Erickson, MD. In *Advanced techniques of hypnosis and therapy: Selected papers of Milton H. Erickson, MD,* New York: Grune & Stratton.

Haley, J. (1973). *Uncommon therapy: The psychiatric techniques of Milton H. Erickson.* New York: W.W. Norton.

Haley, J. (1976a). Development of a theory: A history of a research project. In C. Sluzki & D. Ransom (Eds.), *Double bind: The foundation of the communicational approach to the family.* New York: Grune & Stratton.

Haley, J. (1976b). *Problem-solving therapy.* San Francisco: Jossey Bass.

Heatherton, T., & Polivy, J. (1992). Chronic dieting and eating disorders: A spiral model. In J. Crowther, D. Tennenbaum, S. Hobfoll, & M. Stephens (Eds.), *The etiology of bulimia nervosa: The individual and familial context* (pp. 133–155). Washington, DC: Hemisphere.

Herzog, D., Keller, M., Sacks, N., Yeh, C., & Lavori, P. (1992). Psychiatric co-morbidity in treatment seeking anorexics and bulimics. *Journal of American Academy of Child and Adolescent Psychiatry, 31,* 810–818.

Hester, R., & Miller, W. (1989). Self control training. In R. Hester & W. Miller (Eds.), *Handbook of alcoholism treatment approaches* (pp. 141–148). New York: Pergamon Press.

Hoffman, L. (1985). Beyond power and control: Toward a "second order" family systems therapy. *Family Systems Medicine, 3,* 381–396.

Johnson, C. (1991). Treatment of eating disordered patients with borderline and false-self/narcissistic disorders. In C. Johnson (Ed.), *Psychodynamic treatment of anorexia nervosa and bulimia* (pp. 165–193). New York: Guilford Press.

Johnson, C., & Maddi, I. (1986). The etiology of bulimia: A biopsychosocial perspective. In S. Feinstein, J. Esman, A. Looney, A. Schwartzberg, A. Sorosky, & M. Sugar (Eds.), *Adolescent psychiatry* (Vol. 13, pp. 253–273). Chicago: University of Chicago Press.

Johnson, W., & Brief, D. (1983). Bulimia. *Behavioral Medicine Update, 4,* 16–21.

Kent, J., & Clopton, J. (1992). Bulimic women's perceptions of their family relationships. *Journal of Clinical Psychology, 48,* 281–287.

Koss, M., & Butcher, J. (1986). Research on brief psychotherapy. In S. Garfield & A. Bergin (Eds.), *Handbook of psychotherapy and behavior change* (3rd ed., pp. 627–670). New York: Wiley.

Lambley, P., & Scott, D. (1988). An overview of bulimia nervosa. In D. Scott (Ed.), *Anorexia and bulimia nervosa: Practical approaches* (pp. 87–105). New York: New York University Press.

Langer, E. (1989). *Mindfulness.* Reading, MA: Addison-Wesley.

Levenkron, S. (1982). *Treating and overcoming anorexia nervosa.* New York: Charles Scribner's Sons.

Love, S., Ollendick, T., Johnson, C., & Schlesinger, S. (1985). A preliminary report of the prediction of bulimic behaviors: A social learning analysis. *Bulletin of the Society of Psychologists in Addictive Behaviors, 4,* 93–101.

McFarland, B., & Baker-Baumann, T. (1990). *Shame and body image.* Pompano Beach, Florida: Health Communications.

Madanes, C. (1981). *Strategic family therapy.* San Francisco: Jossey-Bass.

Maslow, A. (1966). *The psychology of science: A reconnaissance.* New York: Harper-Collins.

Miller, S. (1992a). The symptoms of solution. *Journal of Strategic and Systemic Therapies, 11,* 1–11.

Miller S. (1992b, April). Material presented during supervision, Cincinnati, Ohio.

Miller, S. (1993, September). Workshop handouts entitled: Step II: Negotiating "well formed" treatment goals. Cincinatti, Ohio.

Miller, W. (1985). Motivation for treatment: A review with special emphasis on alcoholism. *Psychological Bulletin, 98,* 84–107.

Miller, W. (1989). Increasing motivation for change. In R. Hester & W. Miller (Eds.), *Handbook of alcoholism treatment approaches* (pp. 67–80). New York: Pergammon Press.

Miller, W., & Rollnick, S. (1991). *Motivational interviewing: Preparing people to change addictive behavior.* New York: Guilford Press.

Minuchin, S., Rosman, B., & Baker, L. (1978). *Psychosomatic families.* Cambridge, MA: Harvard University Press.

Molnar, A., & deShazer, S. (1987). Solution focused therapy: Toward the identification of therapeutic tasks. *Journal of Marital and Family Therapy, 13,* 349–358.

Noonan, R. (1973). A follow-up of pretherapy dropouts. *Journal of Community Psychology, 1,* 43–45.

O'Hanlon, W. (1987). *Taproots: The underlying principles of Milton Erickson's therapy and hypnosis.* New York: W.W. Norton.

O'Hanlon, W. (1993). Possibility therapy: From iatrogenic injury to iatrogenic healing. In S. Gilligan & R. Price (Eds.), *Therapeutic conversations,* (pp. 3–17). New York: W.W. Norton.

O'Hanlon, W., & Weiner-Davis, M. (1989). *In search of solutions: A new direction in psychotherapy.* New York: W.W. Norton.

O'Hanlon, W., & Wilk, J. (1987). *Shifting contexts: The generation of effective psychotherapy.* New York: Guilford Press.

Orlinsky, D., & Howard, K. (1986) Process and outcome in psychotherapy. In S. Garfield & A. Bergin (Eds.), *Handbook of psychotherapy and behavior change* (3rd ed., pp. 311–381). New York: Wiley.

Polivy, J., Heatherton, T., & Herman, C. (1988). Self esteem, restraint, and eating behavior. *Journal of Abnormal Psychology, 97,* 354–356.

Prochaska, J., & DiClemente, C. (1982, Fall). Transtheoretical therapy: Toward a more integrative model of change. *Psychotherapy Theory, Research and Practice, 19*(3), 212–216.

Root, M., Fallon, P., & Friedrich, W. (1986). *Bulimia: A systems approach to treatment.* New York: W.W. Norton.

Rosen, J., Gross, J., & Vara, L. (1987). Psychological adjustment of adolescents attempting to lose or gain weight. *Journal of Consulting and Clinical Psychology, 55,* 742–747.

Rosenthal, R., & Jacobsen, L. (1968). *Pygmalion in the classroom: Teacher expectation and pupil's intellectual development.* Troy, MO: Holt, Rinehart & Winston.

Schwartz, D., Thompson, M., Johnson, C. (1981). Anorexia nervosa and bulimia: The sociocultural context. *International Journal of Eating Disorders, 1,* 20–36.

Seeman, J. (1989). Toward a model of positive health. *American Psychologist, 44,* 343–364.

Selvini-Palazzoli, M. (1974). *Self-starvation: From the intrapsychic to the transpersonal approach to anorexia nervosa* (Arnol Pomerans, Trans.). London: Chaucer.

Selvini-Palazzoli, M. (1978). *Self-starvation: From individual to family therapy in the treatment of anorexia nervosa.* New York: Aronson.

Siegel, B. (1986). *Love, medicine & miracles: Lessons learned about self-healing from a surgeon's experience with exceptional patients.* New York: HarperCollins.

Slade, P. (1982). Towards a functional analysis of anorexia nervosa and bulimia nervosa. *British Journal of Clinical Psychology, 21,* 167–179.

Smith, M., Glass, G., & Miller, T. (1980). *The benefits of psychotherapy.* Baltimore, MD: Johns Hopkins University Press.

Steiger, H., Leung, T., & Freedom, J. (1993). Comorbid features in bulimics before and after therapy: Are they explained by Axis II diagnoses, secondary effects of bulimia, or both? *Comprehensive Psychiatry, 34,* 45–53.

Striegel-Moore, R., Silberstein, L., & Rodin, J. (1986). Toward an understanding of risk factors in bulimia. *American Psychologist, 41*(3), 246–263.

Strober, M., Salkin, B., Burroughs, J., & Morrell, W. (1982). Validity of the bulimia-restricter distinction in anorexia nervosa: Parental personality characteristics and family psychiatric morbidity. *Journal of Nervous and Mental Disease, 170,* 345–351.

Swift, W., Bushnell, M., Hanson, P., & Logemann, T. (1986). Self-concept in adolescent anorexics. *Journal of the American Academy of Child Psychiatry, 25,* 826–835.

Talmon, M. (1990). *Single-session therapy: Maximizing the effect of the first (and often only) therapeutic encounter.* San Francisco: Jossey Bass.

Vitousek, K., Daly, J., & Heiser, C. (1991). Reconstructing the internal world of the eating disordered individual: Overcoming denial and distortion in self-report. *International Journal of Eating Disorders, 10,* 647–666.

Waller, J., Kaufman, M., & Deutsch, F. (1940). Anorexia nervosa: Psychosomatic entity. *Psychosomatic Medicine, 2,* 3–16.

Watzlawick, P. (1984). *The invented reality.* New York: W.W. Norton.

Watzlawick, P., Weakland, J., & Fisch, R. (1974). *Change: Principles of problem formation and problem resolution.* New York: W.W. Norton.

Weakland, J. (1993). Conversation. But what kind? In S. Gilligan & S. Reese (Eds.), *Therapeutic conversations* (pp. 136–146). New York: W.W. Norton.

Weakland, J., Fisch, R., Watzlawick, P., & Bodin, A. (1974). Brief therapy: Focused problem resolution. *Family Process, 13,* 141–168.

Weil, A. (1988). *Health and healing.* Boston: Houghton Mifflin.

Weiner-Davis, M. (1993). Pro-constructed realities. In S. Gilligan & S. Reese (Eds.), *Therapeutic conversations* (pp.149–157). New York: W.W. Norton.

Weiner-Davis, M., deShazer, S., & Gingerich, W. (1987). Constructing the therapeutic solution by building on pre-treatment change—An exploratory study. *Journal of Marital and Family Therapy, 13*(4), 359–363.

White, M., & Epston, D. (1990). *Narrative means to therapeutic ends.* New York: W.W. Norton.

Wooley, S., & Kearney-Cooke, A. (1986). Intensive treatment of bulimia and body image disturbance. In K. Brownell & J. Foreyt (Eds.), *Handbook of eating disorders* (pp. 476–501). New York: Basic Books.

Yalom, I. (1975). *The theory and practice of group psychotherapy* (2nd ed.). New York: Basic Books.

Yates, A. (1990). Current perspectives on the eating disorders: II. Treatment, outcome, and research directions. *Journal of the American Academy of Child and Adolescent Psychiatry, 29,* 1–9.

Yates, A. (1992). Biologic considerations in the etiology of eating disorders. *Pediatric Annals, 21,* 741–744.

Index